Infused Water

150 Delicious & Nutritious Recipes

Stephanie Bennett

INTRODUCTION _____ 1
- Infused Water Benefits _____ 1
- Iced Tea Benefits _____ 2
- Juicing Benefits _____ 3

INFUSED WATER RECIPES _____ 5
- Aloe Lemon Water _____ 5
- Apple Cinnamon Water _____ 5
- Apple, Pear and Ginger Delight _____ 6
- Autumn Flavor _____ 6
- Autumn Wind _____ 7
- Beach Breeze _____ 8
- Berry and Orange Fruit Infused Ice Cubes _____ 8
- Berry, Rose Petal and Vanilla _____ 9
- Black Currant Water _____ 10
- Blackberry, Kiwi and Lemon _____ 10
- Blueberry and Apple Water _____ 11
- Blueberry Lavender Infused Water _____ 12
- Cantaloupe-Grape Delight _____ 12
- Carrot and Ginger Water _____ 13
- Cherry Cucumber Refresher _____ 14
- Cherry Limeade _____ 14
- Cherry-Mint Water _____ 15
- Chilling Orange Treat _____ 15
- Cilantro, Cucumber and Melon _____ 16
- Cinnamon Melon Delight _____ 17
- Citrus and Cranberry Drink _____ 17
- Citrus Awakening _____ 18
- Citrus Mint Soda _____ 19
- Citrus-Cilantro Delight _____ 19
- Citrus-Pear Delight _____ 20
- Cooling Mint and Apricot Water _____ 21
- Cranberry Grapefruit Water _____ 21
- Cucumber Lavender Delight _____ 22
- Cucumber Spearmint Water _____ 22
- Fennel-Lemon Water _____ 23
- Flavorful Chiller _____ 24
- Fresh Flight _____ 24
- Fruit-Rosemary Delight _____ 25
- Ginger-Mango Delight _____ 26
- Grape and Blood Orange Water _____ 26
- Grapefruit-Lavender Delight _____ 27

Grapefruit-Pineapple Fizz	28
Grape-Green Tea	28
Green Tea and Tangerine	29
Herbed Tomato Water	29
Herby Grapefruit Water	30
Herby Spring Delight	31
Hibiscus Pineapple Delight	31
Honeydew Agua Fresca	32
Honeydew Date Water	33
Infused Cleanser	34
Jalapeno Cilantro Lemonade	34
Key Lime and Plum Water	35
Kiwi and Lychee Fizz	35
Kiwi and Sage Water	36
Lemongrass Apple Water	37
Lime, Tea and Agave Cleanse	37
Mango and Sugarcane Infused Water	38
Mango-Mint Water	39
Maple Cranberry Drink	39
Melon-Blueberry Fizz	40
Mint Pineapple Treat	40
Mint-Cherry Blast	41
Minty Watermelon Delight	42
Orange and Black Tea	42
Orange and Lavender	43
Orange Basil Water	43
Orange, Blueberry and Cilantro	44
Orange-Apple Cleanse	45
Papaya Mango Water	45
Pear and Raspberry Delight	46
Pepper Cucumber Delight	47
Peppermint Citrus Cleanse	47
Peppermint Fruit Cleanse	48
Peppermint Lemongrass Water	49
Pineapple and Cantaloupe Water	49
Pineapple Cherry Water	50
Piquant Tomato Water	50
Pom Berry Water	51
Raspberry and Fig Limeade	52
Raspberry Coconut Water	53
Raspberry Peach Cooler	53
Raspberry-Date Water	54

Rhubarb and Apple Water _____ 54
Rose Cantaloupe Refresher _____ 55
Rosemary Delight _____ 56
Rosemary Watermelon Treat _____ 56
Sage and Mint Cucumber _____ 57
Sage Blackberry Water _____ 58
Spicy Stimulator _____ 58
Spring Cantaloupe Water _____ 59
Spring Strawberry Refresher _____ 60
Strawberry Infused Water _____ 60
Strawberry Pineapple Water _____ 61
Strawberry-Mint Fizz _____ 62
Summer Berry Blast _____ 62
Tangerine and Melon Water _____ 63
Tangerine-Ginger Treat _____ 64
Tropical Delight _____ 64
Tropical Paradise _____ 65
Vanilla and Cardamom Orange _____ 65
Vanilla Peach Water _____ 66
Vanilla Plum Water _____ 67
Vanilla Strawberry Water _____ 67
Watermelon Coconut Water _____ 68
Winter Relaxer _____ 69

ICED TEA RECIPES _____ 70

Apple and Lemon Zinger _____ 70
Berrylicious Iced Tea _____ 70
Blackberry Iced Tea _____ 71
Blueberry and Lavender Iced Tea _____ 72
Chamomile and Orange Iced Tea _____ 73
Cherry Iced Tea _____ 73
Chinese Spearmint Iced Tea _____ 74
Cinnamon Pear Iced Tea _____ 75
Citrus and Rosemary Iced Tea _____ 76
Classic Lime Iced Tea _____ 76
Ginger and Mint Iced Tea _____ 77
Ginger Orange Iced Tea _____ 78
Ginger Pineapple Iced Tea _____ 79
Hibiscus and Pomegranate Tea _____ 79
Jasmine Tea with Almond Milk _____ 80
Lemongrass Iced Tea _____ 81
Lemongrass Iced Tea _____ 82

Lime Cucumber Iced Tea 82
Limeade Iced Tea 83
Mango Green Tea 84
Maple Raspberry Tea 84
Mint and Lavender Tea 85
Mint Cucumber Iced Tea 86
Mint Lemonade Iced Tea 87
Mom's Cranberry Tea 87
Orange and Apricot Iced Tea 88
Orange and Lemon Iced Tea 89
Peach and Mango Iced Tea 90
Peach Iced Tea 90
Peppermint Orange Tea 91
Pomegranate Iced Tea 92
Raspberry Basil Iced Tea 92
Raspberry Chamomile Iced Tea 93
Raspberry Grape Iced Tea 94
Raspberry Hibiscus Refresher 95
Rocket Mint Iced Tea 96
Russian-Style Beverage 97
Sparkling Apple Iced Tea 97
Sparkling Apple Tea 98
Sparkling Blueberry Tea 99
Sparkling Cranberry Iced Tea 100
Strawberry Green Tea 100
Strawberry Lemon Iced Tea 101
Strawberry Tangerine Tea 102
Summer Orange Tea 103
Tangerine and Lavender Iced Tea 104
Tangerine Strawberry Iced Tea 104
Tea with Coconut Milk 105
Tropical Iced Tea 106
Vanilla and Jasmine Tea 107

JUICE RECIPES **109**

Anti-Inflammatory Booster 109
Apple Lemonade 109
Apple Pie Juice 110
Apple Pumpkin Juice 111
Apple-Orange Juice 111
Apple-Sprout Treat 112
Artichoke-Carrot Blend 113

Asparagus and Tomato Juice	113
Autumn Flight	114
Autumn Treat	115
Avocado and Apple Juice	116
Beet and Plum Juice	116
Beet Blast	117
Beetroot, Carrot and Lime Juice	118
Berry and Apple Cooler	118
Berry and Carrot Cocktail Drink	119
Berry Grapefruit Mix	120
Black Currant and Sprout Juice	120
Blackberry Lemonade	121
Bloody Mary Juice	122
Bok Choy and Carrot Juice	122
Broccoli and Sprout Juice	123
Brussels Sprouts Juice	124
Cabbage and Broccoli Juice	124
Cabbage and Orange juice	125
Cabbage Apple Crush	126
Cabbage Crush	126
Cabbage Juice with Red Grapes	127
Cantaloupe and Blackberry Juice	128
Carrot and Maca Limeade	128
Carrot and Tangerine Juice	129
Carrot-Fennel Treat	130
Celery Blast	130
Chard and Avocado Blend	131
Chayote Tomato Booster	132
Cherry-Sweet Potato Delight	132
Chili Pepper and Sweet Potato Juice	133
Clean & Green Juice	134
Coconut Apple Pie	134
Cooling Limeade	135
Cranberry Treat	136
Cucumber and Carrot Cocktail	136
Cucumber and Carrot Juice	137
Cucumber Orange Delight	137
Daily Garden Juice	138
Favorite Broccoli Breakfast	139
Fennel Purple Juice	139
Fit Red Treat	140
Fresh Morning Drink	141

Fruit and Cilantro Juice	141
Fruity Detox	142
Fruity Herby Delight	143
Garden Gold	143
Ginger Kale Juice	144
Ginger-Pear Delight	145
Grape and Pear Juice	145
Grape and Sugar Beets	146
Grape Pomeade	147
Grapefruit and Cranberry Delight	147
Grapefruit Mint Juice	148
Grapefruit-Fennel Delight	149
Grape-Melon Blast	149
Green & Yum	150
Green Blast	151
Green Cleanser	151
Green Fanatic	152
Green Forest	153
Green Juice with Dates	153
Green Pear Juice	154
Green Rocket Juice	155
Green Soy Coconut Juice	155
Herb and Lime Juice	156
Herby Energy Drink	157
Hot Beet Juice	157
Hot Swiss Chard Juice	158
Jackfruit Treat	159
Kale and Pear Juice with Grapes	160
Kiwi and Grapefruit Juice	160
Kiwi-Apple Delight	161
Lean Juice	161
Lettuce and Blackberry Delight	162
Lotus Root and Tangerine Juice	163
Mediterranean Juice	163
Melon and Coconut Juice	164
Mint Pineapple Juice	165
Minty Beets with Fruits	165
Minty Watermelon Treat	166
Mouth-Watering Drink	166
Orange Blueberry Blast	167
Orange Invigoration	168
Orange-Carrot Crush	168

Papaya and Strawberry Juice	169
Party Ginger Drink	169
Peach and Raspberry Juice	170
Pear and Lettuce Juice	171
Pear and Yam Delight	172
Pear-Cabbage Juice	172
Pear-Tangerine Blast	173
Pineapple Blueberry Juice	174
Pineapple Melon Juice	174
Pineapple-Ginger Cleanser	175
Plum and Pear Juice	176
Plum Tomato Juice	176
Pomegranate Watermelon Juice	177
Post-Workout Revitalizer	178
Protein Spirulina Limeade	178
Purple Kale and Carrot Juice	179
Radicchio and Lemon Delight	180
Radish and Pepper Juice	180
Rainbow Juice	181
Red Cabbage Juice	182
Root Vegetable Detox	182
Simple Detoxing Blend	183
Simple Fruit and Veggie Juice	183
SImple Rejuvinator	184
Sip of India	185
Soft Summer Juice	185
Spice Blast	186
Spicy Dandelion Greens Juice	187
Spicy Root Vegetable Juice	187
Spicy Tangy Cucumber Juice	188
Spinach Power	189
Spinach-Carrot Juice	189
Summer Frostbite	190
Summertime Mint Juice	191
Sweet Cauliflower Delight	191
Sweet Potato Treat	192
Take-off	193
Tangerine and Ginger Juice	193
Tangerine and Root Vegetables with Greens	194
Tangerine Delight	195
Tangerine Turmeric Juice	195
Tangerine-Carrot Crush	196

Tropical Green Delight	197
Tropical Mint Blast	197
Ultimate Tomato Juice	198
Ultra Green Delight	199
Ultra Winter Mix	199
Uplifting Spicy Juice	200
Veggie Stimulator	201
Veggie-Lime Delight	202
Veggie-Sprout Blast	202
Watermelon and Ginger Juice	203
Wheatgrass and Arugula Juice	203
Wheatgrass Tangy Delight	204
Winter Blast	205
Winter Treasure	205
Yam-Pineapple Delight	206
Yam-Tangerine Refresh	207
Yummy Purple Juice	207

Endnote — *209*

INTRODUCTION

Your reasons for picking up this book are your own. Maybe you just want a more balanced diet with a wide spectrum of nutrients and minerals, maybe you're looking to do a juice cleanse, maybe you're looking to hydrate and are bored of bland old water, maybe you are a busy person who doesn't have the time to sit and eat for hours every day, or maybe you just like to gulp some delicious liquids. Whatever your reasons, you're in the right place.

The recipes in this book should keep you satisfied for years to come, and I hope you find a few recipes that you enjoy for life!

INFUSED WATER BENEFITS

Homemade infused water is a great alternative to regular water. Infused water is easy to make, delicious, and nutritious

This book contains about 100 basic infused water recipes, and once you've tried them, treat these recipes as a blank canvas and start making your own combinations! The possibilities are limitless! Certain fruits, vegetables, and herbs are better than others when it comes to infusion, and you will know which ones work, and which ones you like best when you start making infused water. Here's what you will need to get started:

Tools. Having a dedicated fruit infusion bottle or pitcher sure makes the process easier, but any old container will do in a pinch. You can easily find these in stores, or online on amazon. You will also need a tool to mash the ingredients, but a tool for that will surely be present in your kitchen already.

Ingredients. A little obvious, but you cannot create infused water without the necessary fruit, vegetables, and herbs. As for the combinations, feel free to experiment once you get a hang of the process.

Patience. Infused water usually takes a few hours to be complete, so keep that in mind.

All right, no point wasting any more time in this section. Let's jump right into the recipes!

ICED TEA BENEFITS

Iced tea is insanely delicious and nutritious, and a great way to beat the heat during a hot summer day. Iced tea is quite beneficial for the health too, if made at home with healthy ingredients. Some of these benefits are:

1. **Sugar Intake Reduction:** Unsweetened iced tea is the best kind of iced tea, and when you're craving a refreshing drink, drink this instead of a sweet alternative.

2. **Heart-Health:** Iced tea is known to reduce the risk of heart attack.
3. **Anti-Cancer:** Iced tea reduces the risk of cancer!
4. **Brain Health:** Iced tea has small amounts of caffeine, which can enhance mental alertness and performance, when you need it. There are herbal teas that contain no caffeine too.
5. **Antioxidants.** Iced tea is rich in antioxidants, which have innumerable health benefits.
6. **Source of minerals.** Black and green tea are both loaded with healthy minerals, vitamins, and flavonoids.

JUICING BENEFITS

It is an established fact that juicing has great benefits for health. In today's world, getting a balanced diet with the right amount of minerals, nutrients, and fiber can be hard. There is a reason why food supplements like multivitamin tablets are so popular today. However, tablets are boring, unnatural, and don't usually taste good. Everything your body needs, the nature provides in some way or the other, all you need to do is extract that essence and gulp it up!

Juicing also saves time, assuming you have the right machinery for it. A significant portion of the working class today relies on liquid breakfast, and juices are great breakfasts.

Juicing is great for your metabolism too, and going on a juice diet for a few days can give a much-needed reprieve to your digestive system.

One of the most common reasons why people go on a juice diet is detoxification. A juice cleanse is a great way to flush the toxins from your body, and lose weight by creating a calorie deficit at the same time.

Pretty much every juice in this book is going to be highly beneficial for you, assuming you aren't having any underlying health conditions. Diabetics, for example, should not consume juices that are rich in sugar. So, if you're having a health condition, make sure you consult your physician before going on a juice diet.

INFUSED WATER RECIPES

ALOE LEMON WATER

Time to prepare: Approximately ten minutes

Yield: 4 Servings

What You'll Need:

- 1 lemon, squeezed
- 4 tablespoons Aloe gel

Procedure:

1. Combine all ingredientsin your blender or a food processor.
2. Serve over ice and enjoy!

APPLE CINNAMON WATER

Time to prepare: Approximately fifteen minutes

Yield: 4 Servings

What You'll Need:

- 1 red apple, cored, and diced
- 1 vanilla bean

- 2 cinnamon sticks

Procedure:

1. Simply infuse the ingredients in boiling water for five to ten minutes. Allow it to cool and move to a refrigerator.
2. Pour the fruit infused water into a jar and leave in your refrigerator overnight.

APPLE, PEAR AND GINGER DELIGHT

Time to prepare: Approximately ten minutes

Yield: 4 Servings

What You'll Need:

- 1 apple, cored and diced
- 1 pear, cored and diced
- 1-inch fresh ginger root, peeled and chopped

Procedure:

1. Simply put in ingredients to the bottle and then fill it up with filtered or seltzer water.
2. Now keep it in your fridge. You will be able to refill the water a few times. Enjoy!

AUTUMN FLAVOR

Time to prepare: **Approximately ten minutes**

Yield: 4 Servings

What You'll Need:

- 1 apple, cored
- 1 cinnamon
- 4-5 cloves

Procedure:

1. Put the ingredients in a bottle. Fill it with water.

Best enjoyed chilled.

AUTUMN WIND

Time to prepare: **Approximately ten minutes**

Yield: 4 Servings

What You'll Need:

- 1 pear thinly cut
- 1 tangerine, peeled and slice into slices
- 1 teaspoon All Spice Berries
- 2 tablespoons dried cherries

Procedure:

1. Put your ingredients in a pitcher.

2. Next, fill up with water; allow it to sit for approximately 3 hours before drinking.

BEACH BREEZE

Time to prepare: Approximately ten minutes

Yield: 4 Servings

What You'll Need:

- 1/2 cup watermelon, cubed
- Filtered watermelon
- Pre-steeped Hibiscus tea leaves

Procedure:

1. Mix all the above ingredients in a glass bottle or a mason jar.
2. Fill it with water and stir until blended well.
3. Keep in a fridge before you serve. Enjoy!

BERRY AND ORANGE FRUIT INFUSED ICE CUBES

Time to prepare: Approximately ten minutes

Yield: 6 Servings

What You'll Need:

- 1 cup frozen cherries
- 2 mandarin oranges
- 2 tablespoons dried raisins
- 4 cups water

Procedure:

1. Peel your mandarin oranges.
2. In a pan, bring mandarin orange peel and water to its boiling point. Set aside to cool.
3. Then cut mandarin oranges into little cubes. Move them to silicone ice cube trays. Put in raisins and cherries. Fill the ice cube trays with reserved water.
4. Put the trays into the freezer until the cubes frozen. Place the cubes into glasses, fill with water and enjoy!

BERRY, ROSE PETAL AND VANILLA

Time to prepare: Approximately ten minutes

Yield: 4 Servings

What You'll Need:

- 1 big vanilla bean, cut along the length
- 5-6 fresh or frozen blackberries
- 7-8 dried pink rose petals

Procedure:

1. Put your ingredients into a pitcher and fill with cold filtered water.
2. Let the water stay in your fridge overnight.
3. Strain the water and keep the pitcher in your refrigerator. Use within a few days.

BLACK CURRANT WATER

Time to prepare: Approximately ten minutes

Yield: 4 Servings

What You'll Need:

- 1 pint water
- 1 tablespoon apple cider vinegar
- 4 basil leaves
- 1/2 cup pineapple
- 6-7 black currants

Procedure:

1. Put all the ingredients into your pitcher or a mason jar. Move to a fridge.
2. The longer your drink sits, the better it tastes!

BLACKBERRY, KIWI AND LEMON

Time to prepare: Approximately ten minutes

Yield: 4 Servings

What You'll Need:

- 1 kiwi, peeled and quartered
- 1 lemon, cut into wedges
- 3-4 blackberries

Procedure:

1. Move the ingredients to a gallon-size glass jar.
2. Pour in filtered water and mix to blend well. Enjoy with ice!

BLUEBERRY AND APPLE WATER

Time to prepare: Approximately ten minutes

Yield: 2 Servings

What You'll Need:

- 1 green apple, cored and quartered
- 1/2 cup blueberries, gently scrunched
- Filtered or sparkling water

Procedure:

1. Put in the fruits to a glass container or a pitcher. Put in water and stir with your wooden spoon.

2. Allow the fruit infused water to stand minimum 4 hours in a fridge. The longer, the better. Serve completely chilled with straws.

BLUEBERRY LAVENDER INFUSED WATER

Time to prepare: Approximately forty minutes

Yield: 8 Servings

What You'll Need:

- 1/2 cup blueberries
- 4 cups water
- Lavender edible flowers

Procedure:

1. Put in the ingredients to a pitcher.
2. Next, chill the water for minimum half an hour.
3. Strain, pour over ice cubes, before you serve.

CANTALOUPE-GRAPE DELIGHT

Time to prepare: Approximately ten minutes

Yield: 4 Servings

What You'll Need:

- 1 vanilla bean

- Filtered water
- 1/2 cup cantaloupe, cubed
- 1-2 cinnamon sticks
- 5-6 grapes, gently scrunched

Procedure:

1. Place the ingredients into a mason jar or a gallon jug. Stir gently in order to blend well.
2. Keep in your fridge for maximum a week. Stay cool and hydrated!

CARROT AND GINGER WATER

Time to prepare: Approximately ten minutes

Yield: 6 Servings

What You'll Need:

- 1 sprig rosemary
- 1-inch ginger root, peeled and cut
- 2 carrots, chopped
- Sparkling plain water

Procedure:

1. Put all the above ingredients in a pitcher.
2. You can refill the pitcher a few times.

CHERRY CUCUMBER REFRESHER

Time to prepare: Approximately ten minutes

Yield: 2 Servings

What You'll Need:

- 1 cucumber, peeled and cut
- 1 handful cherries
- 1 tablespoon fresh cilantro
- 3 cups water

Procedure:

1. Put your ingredients in a pitcher. Allow to sit for a few hours to release flavors
2. Serve thoroughly chilled and enjoy all day long!

CHERRY LIMEADE

Time to prepare: Approximately ten minutes

Yield: 2 Servings

What You'll Need:

- 1 cup fresh cherries, pitted
- 2 limes, thinly cut
- Agave syrup, to taste

Procedure:

1. Put the ingredients in your mason jar.
2. Finally, serve completely chilled.

CHERRY-MINT WATER

Time to prepare: Approximately ten minutes

Yield: 2 Servings

What You'll Need:

- 8 fresh cherries, pitted and halved
- Water
- 1/4 cup mint leaves

Procedure:

1. Mash the cherries and move to a mason jar. Fill the jar with water; shake it thoroughly.
2. Serve completely chilled and enjoy!

CHILLING ORANGE TREAT

Time to prepare: Approximately fifteen minutes

Yield: 4 Servings

What You'll Need:

- 1 cup fresh orange juice
- 1 tablespoon ground fresh ginger

- 2 cups cold water
- 3 cups sparkling water
- Orange slices, for decoration

Procedure:

1. Mix water, orange juice, and fresh ginger in your blender; pulse until everything is well mixed.
2. Strain mixture over a pitcher. Pour in sparkling water just before you serve.
3. Serve over ice and decorate with orange slices.

CILANTRO, CUCUMBER AND MELON

Time to prepare: **Approximately ten minutes**

Yield: **2 Servings**

What You'll Need:

- 1 cucumber, cut
- 1 tablespoon fresh cilantro
- 1 tablespoon fresh parsley
- Filtered water
- 1/2 cup melon, cubed
- 3-4 cardamom pods

Procedure:

1. Put the ingredients in a glass bottle.

2. Allow to sit for a few hours in your refrigerator.

CINNAMON MELON DELIGHT

Time to prepare: Approximately ten minutes

Yield: 4 Servings

What You'll Need:

- 1 cup cantaloupe, cubed
- 1 cup honeydew, cubed
- 1 cup watermelon, cubed
- 2 quarts filtered water
- 2 sticks cinnamon

Procedure:

1. Put in your ingredients to a mason jar or a bottle. Allow to sit for a few hours in the refrigerator.
2. Serve over ice or completely chilled.

CITRUS AND CRANBERRY DRINK

Time to prepare: Approximately ten minutes

Yield: 4 Servings

What You'll Need:

- 16 ounces water

- 1/2 cup cranberries
- 1/2 lime, cut
- 1/2 orange

Procedure:

1. Put in the ingredients to a bottle.
2. Allow to sit for approximately 1 hour.

CITRUS AWAKENING

Time to prepare: Approximately fifteen minutes

Yield: 4 Servings

What You'll Need:

- 1 small-sized orange, peeled and cut.
- 6 strawberries, quartered, frozen.
- Pre-steeped Chamomile leaves
- Water

Procedure:

1. Process all ingredients using a blender until it is smooth and consistent.
2. Put in water to a pitcher until full just before you serve.
3. You can put in new water when your bottle or a pitcher is half-way empty.

CITRUS MINT SODA

Time to prepare: Approximately ten minutes

Yield: 4 Servings

What You'll Need:

- 1 cup fresh mint leaves
- 1 grapefruit, cut
- 1 lemon, cut
- 8 cups club soda

Procedure:

1. Put mint leaves in a pitcher and squeeze them. Put in lemon slices and grapefruit slices.
2. Cover with club soda and move to a fridge. Let sit for a few hours before you serve.

CITRUS-CILANTRO DELIGHT

Time to prepare: Approximately ten minutes

Yield: 4 Servings

What You'll Need:

- 1 grapefruit, peeled and cut
- 1 lemon, peeled and cut
- 1 lime, peeled and cut

- 2 tablespoons fresh cilantro

Procedure:

1. Put the ingredients in a big jar with lid. Fill up the jar with filtered water.
2. Now keep it in your refrigerator; let the water stand for a few hours.
3. Drink completely chilled and enjoy.

CITRUS-PEAR DELIGHT

Time to prepare: Approximately ten minutes

Yield: 4 Servings

What You'll Need:

- 1 Meyer lemon
- 1 pear, cubed
- 1 tangerine
- Fresh cilantro, to taste

Procedure:

1. Put the ingredients in a big glass bottle. Fill it up with cold water and move to a fridge.
2. Pour the water into serving glasses and enjoy!

COOLING MINT AND APRICOT WATER

Time to prepare: Approximately ten minutes

Yield: 4 Servings

What You'll Need:

- 1 sprig mint
- 4 apricot halves, pitted
- 8 peach slices
- Water

Procedure:

1. Simply drop the ingredients in a bottle.
2. Let chill in a fridge for minimum three hours.
3. You will be able to refill your pitcher up to 6 times.

CRANBERRY GRAPEFRUIT WATER

Time to prepare: Approximately ten minutes

Yield: 4 Servings

What You'll Need:

- 1 apple, cored
- 1 grapefruit, cut into wedges
- 1 sprig fresh mint
- 4-5 fresh cranberries

- Water

Procedure:

1. Put the ingredients in a jar or a bottle.
2. The longer the water sits, the better.

CUCUMBER LAVENDER DELIGHT

Time to prepare: Approximately ten minutes

Yield: 2 Servings

What You'll Need:

- 1 cucumber, peeled and cut
- 2 fresh lavender sprigs
- 2 quarts spring water

Procedure:

1. Put in the ingredients to your mason jar.
2. Now place in your fridge until cold before you serve.

CUCUMBER SPEARMINT WATER

Time to prepare: Approximately ten minutes

Yield: 4 Servings

What You'll Need:

- 1 small-sized cucumber, peeled and cut
- 1 small-sized lemon, peeled and cut.
- 6 fresh leaves spearmint gently scrunched
- Filtered water

Procedure:

1. Simply put in the lemon and cucumber to the glass; purée and break them down with a spoon.
2. Next, lightly crush the spearmint leaves to release the natural extracts.
3. Finally, put in filtered water and drink!

FENNEL-LEMON WATER

Time to prepare: Approximately fifteen minutes

Yield: 4 Servings

What You'll Need:

- 1 bunch of fennel seeds
- 1 lemon, peeled
- A few mint leaves

Procedure:

1. Simply smash fennel seeds; put in lemon and mint leaves.

2. Infuse the mixture in 1 liter of boiling water for approximately ten minutes. Let cool and keep in a fridge. Serve completely chilled and enjoy!

FLAVORFUL CHILLER

Time to prepare: Approximately ten minutes

Yield: 4 Servings

What You'll Need:

- 1 cucumber, cut
- 1 cup cubed pineapple
- A few cinnamon sticks
- Cloves, to taste
- Filtered water

Procedure:

1. Place the ingredients into a pitcher. Next, mix thoroughly to blend.
2. Store in your refrigerator to cool before you drink.

FRESH FLIGHT

Time to prepare: Approximately ten minutes

Yield: 4 Servings

What You'll Need:

- 1 cup strawberries, hulled and quartered
- 2 quarts of water
- 1/2 thinly English cucumber, cut
- 1-2 wedges orange

Procedure:

1. Put in the ingredients to your pitcher.
2. Place in your fridge minimum 3 hours in order to allow the ingredients to infuse. Next, strain and discard the solids.
3. Serve with sufficient ice. Store in your fridge for maximum 2 days.

FRUIT-ROSEMARY DELIGHT

Time to prepare: Approximately ten minutes

Yield: 6 Servings

What You'll Need:

- Water
- 1/2 grapefruit, cut
- 1/2 lime, cut
- 2-3 rosemary sprigs

Procedure:

1. Put the grapefruit, lime, and rosemary sprigs in a bottle.
2. Cover with water; allow the drink to stand overnight.
3. Put in some ice right before you serve and enjoy!

GINGER-MANGO DELIGHT

Time to prepare: Approximately ten minutes

Yield: 2 Servings

What You'll Need:

- 1 cup mango, cut
- 1-inch ginger root, peeled and cut
- 3 cups cold filtered water

Procedure:

1. Put the ingredients into a pitcher. Stir and move to a fridge.
2. Serve completely chilled in a pretty glass. Enjoy!

GRAPE AND BLOOD ORANGE WATER

Time to prepare: Approximately ten minutes

Yield: 4 Servings

What You'll Need:

- 1 teaspoon grated ginger root

- Water
- 1/2 medium blood orange
- 1/4 cup grapes

Procedure:

1. Put in all of these components to your pitcher or a mason jar. Stir thoroughly to blend.
2. Put in a fridge for a few hours. Stir before you serve.
3. Serve completely chilled and enjoy!

GRAPEFRUIT-LAVENDER DELIGHT

Time to prepare: Approximately ten minutes

Yield: 2 Servings

What You'll Need:

- 1 grapefruit, peeled and cut
- 2 fresh sprigs lavender, gently scrunched
- 5 fresh mint leaves, gently scrunched

Procedure:

1. Place the ingredients into a big glass bottle. Fill it up with water.
2. Let your water stand in your refrigerator minimum 3 hours to allow the flavors to infuse.
3. Serve completely chilled or with ice cubes.

GRAPEFRUIT-PINEAPPLE FIZZ

Time to prepare: Approximately ten minutes

Yield: 6 Servings

What You'll Need:

- Fizzy water
- 1/2 grapefruit
- 1/2 apple
- 1/2 pineapple

Procedure:

1. Put in the ingredients to your pitcher.
2. Next, place in your fridge overnight for best flavor.

GRAPE-GREEN TEA

Time to prepare: Approximately ten minutes

Yield: 4 Servings

What You'll Need:

- 1-inch ginger root, peeled
- 2 cups grapes
- Pre-steeped Green tea leaves

Procedure:

1. Put all the ingredients into a jar or a bottle. Pour in water.
2. The longer your water sits in your refrigerator, the better it will taste.

GREEN TEA AND TANGERINE

Time to prepare: Approximately ten minutes

Yield: 6 Servings

What You'll Need:

- 1 tangerine, cut
- 10 mint leaves
- 8 cups green tea, brewed

Procedure:

1. Mix your ingredients in a big pitcher or a bottle.
2. Stir thoroughly, and allow the drink to stay in a fridge overnight for the flavors to fuse together.

HERBED TOMATO WATER

Time to prepare: Approximately ten minutes

Yield: 4 Servings

What You'll Need:

- 1 sprig rosemary
- 1 tomato, diced
- 2 quarts water
- 2 sprigs basil

Procedure:

1. In a pitcher, place tomato, herbs, and 1 quart of seltzer. Stir to blend and place in your fridge for two to 4 hours.
2. After this, strain thoroughly, discarding the solids. Put in the second quart of water just before you serve.

HERBY GRAPEFRUIT WATER

Time to prepare: Approximately ten minutes

Yield: 4 Servings

What You'll Need:

- 1 grapefruit, peeled and cut
- 1 sprig rosemary
- 1 tablespoon basil
- 1 tablespoon mint
- 2 cups sparkling water
- 2 tablespoons sage

Procedure:

1. Put grapefruit in the glass; purée it with your spoon.

2. Next, purée the herbs and put in to the prepared grapefruit.
3. Finally, put in sparkling water and serve over ice!

HERBY SPRING DELIGHT

Time to prepare: Approximately ten minutes

Yield: 4 Servings

What You'll Need:

- 6 strawberries, hulled
- 1 tablespoon fresh mint
- Sparkling water
- 1/2 small-sized cucumber, peeled and cut
- 3-4 fresh basil leaves

Procedure:

1. Place the ingredients into a big glass bottle or a jar. Fill it up with water.
2. Serve immediately or keep it in your refrigerator.

HIBISCUS PINEAPPLE DELIGHT

Time to prepare: Approximately ten minutes

Yield: 4 Servings

What You'll Need:

- 1/2 cup pineapple, cubed
- 2 carrots, cut
- A few hibiscus petals

Procedure:

1. Put the ingredients in your bottle. Cover with water and stir until blended well.
2. Serve completely chilled and enjoy!

HONEYDEW AGUA FRESCA

Time to prepare: Approximately ten minutes

Yield: 2 Servings

What You'll Need:

- 1 cup blackberries
- 1 honeydew melon, cut into half
- 3 limes
- 4 cups water

Procedure:

1. Remove seeds from honeydew melon; cut flesh into chunks. Mash it and replace to a sieve.

2. Next, squeeze the juice and pour into a big pitcher; put in water and stir. Chop the lime into thin slices. Put in the lime slices to the pitcher.
3. Pour into serving glasses and decorate with blackberries.

HONEYDEW DATE WATER

Time to prepare: Approximately ten minutes

Yield: 4 Servings

What You'll Need:

- 1 cucumber, cut
- 1 cup honeydew, diced
- 1 tablespoon fresh cilantro
- 1 tablespoon fresh mint
- 1-2 tablespoons dried dates, pitted and roughly chopped

Procedure:

1. Combine the honeydew, cucumber, mint, cilantro and dates in a blender or a food processor. Next, pour the pureed mixture through the sieve.
2. Pour in filtered water. Serve completely chilled.

INFUSED CLEANSER

Time to prepare: Approximately ten minutes

Yield: 2 Servings

What You'll Need:

- 1 cucumber, cut
- 1 lime, cut
- 1/2 cup pomegranate
- Water

Procedure:

1. Put the ingredients in a pitcher or a mason jar.
2. Allow to steep in the refrigerator minimum 2 hours.

JALAPENO CILANTRO LEMONADE

Time to prepare: Approximately ten minutes

Yield: 4 Servings

What You'll Need:

- 1 ½ cups fresh lemon juice
- 1 pint boiling water
- 1/2 cup cilantro, washed and chopped
- 2 jalapenos, seeded and chopped
- Honey to taste

Procedure:

1. To start, pour boiling water over jalapenos and cilantro.
2. Let chill for approximately 4 hours.
3. Put in lemon juice and honey to taste. Enjoy!

KEY LIME AND PLUM WATER

Time to prepare: Approximately ten minutes

Yield: 4 Servings

What You'll Need:

- 1 key lime, cut
- Stevia, to taste
- 4-5 plums

Procedure:

1. Put your ingredients in a mason jar or a pitcher.
2. Use a spoon to slightly purée the ingredients.
3. Finally, pour in sparkling plain water. Stir to blend and serve thoroughly chilled. This beverage can be stored in airtight glasses.

KIWI AND LYCHEE FIZZ

Time to prepare: Approximately ten minutes

Yield: 4 Servings

What You'll Need:

- 2 tablespoons lychee crush
- 3 cups soda
- 3 tablespoons kiwi slices

Procedure:

1. In your blender or a food processor, blend kiwi slices and lychee crush together with 1 cup of soda.
2. Put in rest of the soda water and mix to blend well. Serve over ice cubes.

KIWI AND SAGE WATER

Time to prepare: Approximately ten minutes

Yield: 6 Servings

What You'll Need:

- 1 cucumber, peeled and cut
- 1 tablespoon fresh sage
- 4 kiwis, peeled and quartered
- 6 cups water

Procedure:

1. Put cucumber, kiwi, sage and four cups water in a pitcher. Next, stir until blended and replace to a fridge.
2. Put in rest of the two cups of water just before you serve. Stir and serve completely chilled. Enjoy!

LEMONGRASS APPLE WATER

Time to prepare: Approximately ten minutes

Yield: 4 Servings

What You'll Need:

- 1 cup ice cubes
- 1 green apple, cored and cut
- 1 pint filtered water
- 1 stick cinnamon
- 1 stick sugarcane
- 2 stalks of lemongrass
- 3-5 quarter sized coins of peeled ginger

Procedure:

1. Put all ingredients in a pitcher or a mason jar.
2. Stir to blend.

LIME, TEA AND AGAVE CLEANSE

Time to prepare: Approximately ten minutes

Yield: 4 Servings

What You'll Need:

- 1 lime, cut
- 1 pint water for boiling
- 1 tablespoon agave nectar
- 2 green tea bags

Procedure:

1. Bring water to its boiling point. Next, put in tea bags and lime.
2. Take away the tea bags and put in agave nectar. Move to a refrigerator.

MANGO AND SUGARCANE INFUSED WATER

Time to prepare: **Approximately ten minutes**

Yield: 4 Servings

What You'll Need:

- 1 handful mango chunks
- 1 pint filtered water
- 2 sticks sugarcane

Procedure:

1. Combine the ingredients in a pitcher.
2. Let the beverage chill in your refrigerator minimum 2 hours. Enjoy!

MANGO-MINT WATER

Time to prepare: Approximately ten minutes

Yield: 2 Servings

What You'll Need:

- 1/2 mango, peeled and slice into big chunks
- 2 sprigs of mint
- Soda water

Procedure:

1. Put your ingredients into a mason jar or a bottle.
2. Serve over ice cubes if you wish.

MAPLE CRANBERRY DRINK

Time to prepare: Approximately ten minutes

Yield: 4 Servings

What You'll Need:

- 1 pint filtered water
- 2 tablespoons cranberries

- 3 tablespoons maple syrup
- Key lime, cut

Procedure:

1. Put all the ingredients into a bottle or mason jar.
2. The longer this beverage stands in your refrigerator, the better it will taste.

MELON-BLUEBERRY FIZZ

Time to prepare: **Approximately ten minutes**

Yield: 2 Servings

What You'll Need:

- 1 lemon, cut into wedges
- 1/4 cup blueberries
- 6 cups melon

Procedure:

1. Mix all the above ingredients in a glass bottle.
2. Fill it with seltzer and stir until blended.

MINT PINEAPPLE TREAT

Time to prepare: **Approximately ten minutes**

Yield: 2 Servings

What You'll Need:

- 1/2 cup pineapple chunks
- 1/2 peach, cut
- 1-2 sprigs mint

Procedure:

1. Put all the above ingredients in your pitcher. Pour in cold water and stir.
2. You will be able to refill it for approximately 5 times until the flavor dissipates.
3. To serve: You can put in a couple of frozen pineapple chunks for ice cubes.

MINT-CHERRY BLAST

Time to prepare: Approximately ten minutes

Yield: 4 Servings

What You'll Need:

- 1 lemon, thinly cut
- 1 quart water
- 10 pitted cherries, cut in halves
- 6 mint leaves

Procedure:

1. Put all the ingredients into a mason jar.

2. The longer your water stands in a fridge, the more flavorful your drink will be.

MINTY WATERMELON DELIGHT

Time to prepare: Approximately fifteen minutes

Yield: 4 Servings

What You'll Need:

- 1 cup fresh or frozen watermelon, rind removed and cubed
- 1 lime, peeled and cut
- 1 tablespoon fresh mint leaves, minced

Procedure:

1. Put in cubed watermelon to a bottle. Put in lime, mint leaves, and filtered water to fill.
2. Keep in your refrigerator minimum 4 hours to infuse. Enjoy!

ORANGE AND BLACK TEA

Time to prepare: Approximately ten minutes

Yield: 4 Servings

What You'll Need:

- 1 black tea bag
- 3 mandarin oranges, peeled and slice into half
- Water

Procedure:

1. Put in the ingredients to a bottle. Pour in filtered water; allow it to infuse at room temperature minimum 3 hours.
2. Next, chill in a fridge before you serve.

ORANGE AND LAVENDER

Time to prepare: Approximately ten minutes

Yield: 4 Servings

What You'll Need:

- 1 orange, peeled
- 2 fresh sprigs lavender, gently scrunched

Procedure:

1. Put all the ingredients in a glass bottle. Fill with water.
2. Stir using a wooden spoon and move to a fridge before you serve.

ORANGE BASIL WATER

Time to prepare: Approximately fifteen minutes

Yield: 4 Servings

What You'll Need:

- 1 blood orange, peeled and cut
- 1 tablespoon basil
- 1-inch ginger, peeled

Procedure:

1. Put in the ingredients to a 1/2 gallon glass jar, and fill it up with filtered water.
2. Stir to blend and place in fridge for four to 5 hours. Enjoy!

ORANGE, BLUEBERRY AND CILANTRO

Time to prepare: Approximately ten minutes

Yield: 4 Servings

What You'll Need:

- 1 orange
- 1 tablespoon fresh cilantro
- Water
- 5-6 blueberries

Procedure:

1. Put in the ingredients to a mason jar. Pour in filtered water and stir slowly.
2. Place in your fridge overnight to allow the ingredients to infuse. Enjoy!

ORANGE-APPLE CLEANSE

Time to prepare: Approximately ten minutes

Yield: 4 Servings

What You'll Need:

- 1 fresh orange juice
- 1 moderate-sized apple, cut
- 1 vanilla bean, cut along the length
- 16 ounces filtered water
- 2 tablespoons apple cider vinegar

Procedure:

1. Simply throw all ingredients into your pitcher. Stir to blend.
2. Store in your fridge before you serve. Enjoy!

PAPAYA MANGO WATER

Time to prepare: Approximately ten minutes

Yield: 4 Servings

What You'll Need:

- 1/2 cup papaya chunks
- 1/2 cup mango chunks
- 1/2-inch ginger root, peeled and cut

Procedure:

1. Place the ingredients into a big pitcher. Mush with a back of spoon.
2. Next, fill the pitcher with water. Serve thoroughly chilled. You can refill a few times. Enjoy!

PEAR AND RASPBERRY DELIGHT

Time to prepare: Approximately ten minutes

Yield: 4 Servings

What You'll Need:

- 1 pear, cored and quartered
- 1 tablespoon fresh sage
- 1/2 orange, cut into wedges
- 4-5 raspberries

Procedure:

1. Put your ingredients into the jar or bottle. Put in the water and stir thoroughly.
2. Serve completely chilled or over ice cubes.

PEPPER CUCUMBER DELIGHT

Time to prepare: Approximately ten minutes

Yield: 4 Servings

What You'll Need:

- 1 jalapeno pepper, seeded and cut
- 2 cucumbers, thinly cut

Water

Procedure:

1. Put the ingredients in a big pitcher.
2. Pour over the ice.

PEPPERMINT CITRUS CLEANSE

Time to prepare: Approximately ten minutes

Yield: 4 Servings

What You'll Need:

- 1 cucumber, cut with peels
- 1 lime, cut
- 1 orange, cut
- 1 pint filtered water
- 1 tablespoon freshly grated ginger

- A few peppermint leaves

Procedure:

1. Combine all ingredients in a bottle or a pitcher; place in your fridge for a few hours or overnight.
2. Serve completely chilled and stay hydrated all day long!

PEPPERMINT FRUIT CLEANSE

Time to prepare: Approximately ten minutes

Yield: 4 Servings

What You'll Need:

- 1 ½ cups water
- 1 tangerine, cut
- 2 peppermint leaves
- Water
- 1/2 grapefruit

Procedure:

1. Drop the ingredients in your pitcher.
2. Top with ice cubes and allow it to sit for a few hours in a fridge.
3. You can refill your pitcher up to 4 times. Enjoy!

PEPPERMINT LEMONGRASS WATER

Time to prepare: Approximately ten minutes

Yield: 2 Servings

What You'll Need:

- 1 stalk lemongrass, crushed slightly
- 1 vanilla bean, cut along the length
- 1/4 cup fresh peppermint, chopped

Procedure:

1. Put in the ingredients to a glass container or a pitcher.
2. Pour in water and stir using a wooden spoon.

PINEAPPLE AND CANTALOUPE WATER

Time to prepare: Approximately ten minutes

Yield: 4 Servings

What You'll Need:

- 1 tablespoon fresh mint leaves
- 1 tablespoon fresh sage leaves
- 1/2 cup pineapple chunks
- 1/4 cup cantaloupe chunks

Procedure:

1. Put in the ingredients to a mason jar. Put in the filtered water.
2. Serve completely chilled and enjoy!

PINEAPPLE CHERRY WATER

Time to prepare: **Approximately ten minutes**

Yield: **4 Servings**

What You'll Need:

- 1 apple, cored
- 1/2 pineapple
- 5-6 cherries, pitted

Procedure:

1. Take the rind off your pineapple and cut it into cubes. Move to a gallon-size glass jar. Put in the apple and cherries.
2. Put in filtered water and mix thoroughly to blend.

Enjoy with ice!

PIQUANT TOMATO WATER

Time to prepare: **Approximately ten minutes**

Yield: **4 Servings**

What You'll Need:

- 1 teaspoon kosher salt
- 1/2 cup fresh basil leaves
- 2 shallots, chopped
- 2 tablespoons fresh cilantro leaves
- 2 tablespoons fresh parsley leaves
- 2 tablespoons white wine vinegar
- 2 tomatoes, quartered

Procedure:

1. Puree the ingredients in a food processor until they're crudely chopped.
2. Coat a sieve with cheesecloth and set it over a container.
3. Move tomato mixture to the prepared sieve. Cover and chill overnight.
4. Next, discard solids and serve completely chilled.

POM BERRY WATER

Time to prepare: Approximately ten minutes

Yield: 2 Servings

What You'll Need:

- Water
- 1/2 cup pomegranate

- 1/4 cup fresh raspberries

Procedure:

1. Put your ingredients in a pitcher. Mash them using a spoon.
2. Fill up the pitcher with fresh water. Stir to blend and place in your refrigerator.

RASPBERRY AND FIG LIMEADE

Time to prepare: **Approximately ten minutes**

Yield: **4 Servings**

What You'll Need:

- 1 cup raspberries
- 1 lime, cut
- 2 dried figs, roughly chopped
- 3 basil leaves, roughly chopped
- 8 cups spring water

Procedure:

1. Simply drop all ingredients in your glass jar; now put the lid on top.
2. Put your water in your fridge and let infuse minimum 1 hour.

RASPBERRY COCONUT WATER

Time to prepare: Approximately ten minutes

Yield: 2 Servings

What You'll Need:

- 1 handful raspberries
- 1 small bunch mint
- 2 cups coconut water

Procedure:

1. Put in fresh raspberries to a bottle or a pitcher.
2. Muddle the raspberries to release flavor; put in coconut water and mint.
3. Shake to mix the flavors before you serve.

RASPBERRY PEACH COOLER

Time to prepare: Approximately ten minutes

Yield: 4 Servings

What You'll Need:

- 2 quarts spring water
- 1 small-sized peach, pitted and diced
- A few cinnamon sticks
- 5-6 raspberries

Procedure:

1. Put in the ingredients to a pitcher. Now chill it at least half an hour.
2. To serve: pour it over ice cubes in serving glasses. Next, keep your water in your refrigerator until serving time.

RASPBERRY-DATE WATER

Time to prepare: **Approximately ten minutes**

Yield: **4 Servings**

What You'll Need:

- 1 cup raspberries
- 1 lemon, cut
- 2 dried Medjool dates
- 8 cups filtered water

Procedure:

1. Put in the ingredients to a 1-gallon clean glass jar with lid.
2. Move this amazing beverage to your fridge and let infuse for a few hours. Enjoy!

RHUBARB AND APPLE WATER

Time to prepare: **Approximately ten minutes**

Yield: 4 Servings

What You'll Need:

- 1 Granny Smith apple, cored and cut
- 1 rhubarb, cut
- 1 stick cinnamon
- 1 vanilla bean, slice along the length
- Anise seed, to taste

Procedure:

1. Put the ingredients in a carafe and fill with water. Place in your fridge until ready to serve.
2. Keep it for approximately 2 days in your fridge. Refill a few times until flavor dissipates.

ROSE CANTALOUPE REFRESHER

Time to prepare: Approximately ten minutes

Yield: 2 Servings

What You'll Need:

- 1 cup cantaloupe pieces
- 1 tablespoon tarragon
- A few edible rose petals
- 2 quarts filtered water
- 1/2 fennel bulb, thinly cut

Procedure:

1. Put in the ingredients to big glass bottles.
2. You can refill your water a few times, and then, let it infuse over once more.
3. Enjoy this aromatic and refreshing beverage!

ROSEMARY DELIGHT

Time to prepare: **Approximately ten minutes**

Yield: **4 Servings**

What You'll Need:

- 1 fresh sprig rosemary, gently scrunched
- 1/2 grapefruit, cut into wedges
- 1/2 kiwi fruit, peeled and cut

Procedure:

1. Place the ingredients into a big jar or a pitcher. Pour in coconut water and stir until blended.
2. Finally, place in your fridge overnight for best flavor. The water can be stored in a mason jar, water bottle, etc.

ROSEMARY WATERMELON TREAT

Time to prepare: **Approximately ten minutes**

Yield: 4 Servings

What You'll Need:

- 1 sprig mint
- 1 sprig rosemary
- 1/4 cup watermelon chunks
- 5-6 raspberries

Procedure:

1. Mix all the above ingredients in a big glass jar. Fill the jar with spring water of choice.
2. Allow to sit for half an hour before enjoying. Serve over ice cubes. Happy drinking!

SAGE AND MINT CUCUMBER

Time to prepare: Approximately fifteen minutes

Yield: 4 Servings

What You'll Need:

- 1 cucumber, cut
- 2 lemons, peeled and cut
- Fresh mint, to taste
- Sage, to taste

Procedure:

1. Put in the ingredients to a gallon size glass jar.
2. Pour in filtered water and stir slowly.
3. Place in your fridge overnight in order to develop flavors. Enjoy!

SAGE BLACKBERRY WATER

Time to prepare: Approximately ten minutes

Yield: 4 Servings

What You'll Need:

- 1 tablespoon sage
- 1/2 cup blackberry
- 1/2-inch ginger root

Procedure:

1. Put in all ingredients to your pitcher or a mason jar.
2. Pour in your favorite spring water or coconut water.
3. Stir your fruit infused water, cover with a lid and move it to the fridge; allow it to sit overnight for the best flavor. You should drink it within 2-3 days. Enjoy!

SPICY STIMULATOR

Time to prepare: Approximately ten minutes

Yield: 2 Servings

What You'll Need:

- 1 cucumber, peeled and cut along the length
- 1 lemon, cut
- 1 teaspoon fresh ginger root, slivered
- 2 cups water
- 4 fresh mint leaves, gently scrunched

Procedure:

1. Mix all the above ingredients.
2. You must be able to refill your bottle with flavored water for one to three times before you have to replace ingredients. Enjoy!

SPRING CANTALOUPE WATER

Time to prepare: Approximately ten minutes

Yield: 4 Servings

What You'll Need:

- 1 cup cantaloupe, cubed
- 1 cup raspberries, hulled and quartered
- 2 quarts spring water

Procedure:

1. Put in the raspberries and cantaloupe to a mason jar or your pitcher.

2. Pour spring water over it and place in your fridge for quite a few hours. Serve over ice cubes.
3. If you prefer your beverage sweet, add a small amount of agave nectar.

SPRING STRAWBERRY REFRESHER

Time to prepare: Approximately ten minutes

Yield: 4 Servings

What You'll Need:

- 1 sprig fresh mint
- 1/2 cup mango, chunks
- 4-5 strawberries, hulled and halved

Procedure:

1. Put mint leaves in a pitcher and squeeze them using the back of a regular spoon. Put in mango and strawberries.
2. Cover with spring water or coconut water; move to a fridge for a few hours before you serve.

STRAWBERRY INFUSED WATER

Time to prepare: Approximately fifteen minutes

Yield: 4 Servings

What You'll Need:

- 2 limes, squeezed
- 4 cups water
- 4 tablespoons molasses
- 6 cups strawberries, hulled

Procedure:

1. Mix water and molasses, and stir meticulously until it is well blended.
2. Mix strawberries in a blender.
3. Put in strawberry puree to molasses mixture; put in lime juice.
4. Finally, stir thoroughly before you serve. The water helps you improve overall health

STRAWBERRY PINEAPPLE WATER

Time to prepare: Approximately ten minutes

Yield: 6 Servings

What You'll Need:

- 1 cup frozen strawberries
- 1 lemon, peeled and cut
- 1/2 cup pineapple chunks
- 4 cups water

Procedure:

1. Put in all ingredients to a bottle. Stir to blend.
2. Serve with frozen strawberries as ice cubes and enjoy!

STRAWBERRY-MINT FIZZ

Time to prepare: Approximately ten minutes

Yield: 4 Servings

What You'll Need:

- 1 small-sized cucumber, cut
- 3 strawberries, cut
- 5 fresh mint leaves
- Sparkling water

Procedure:

1. Mix the ingredients in a big mason jar. Next, stir thoroughly.
2. Let the drink sit in a fridge overnight.

SUMMER BERRY BLAST

Time to prepare: Approximately ten minutes

Yield: 2 Servings

What You'll Need:

- Sparkling water
- 5-6 strawberries, hulled and quartered
- 5-6 blackberries, gently scrunched brambles
- 5-6 blueberries, halved

Procedure:

1. First, simply put in the berries to a large-sized glass; purée it using a muddler.
2. Finally, put in sparkling water and drink!

TANGERINE AND MELON WATER

Time to prepare: Approximately ten minutes

Yield: 4 Servings

What You'll Need:

- 1 mango, pitted and cut
- 1 tangerine, thinly cut
- 2 quarts filtered water
- 3 basil leaves, roughly chopped

Procedure:

1. Put in your tangerine, mango, filtered water, and basil leaves to a pitcher.
2. Pour the water over top and chill before you serve.
3. Serve over ice cubes.

TANGERINE-GINGER TREAT

Time to prepare: Approximately ten minutes

Yield: 4 Servings

What You'll Need:

- 1-inch piece ginger, peeled and cut
- 2 quarts filtered or spring water
- 1/2 cup tangerine, peeled and cut
- 1/2 cup pineapple, crushed

Procedure:

1. Put in the ingredients to your pitcher.
2. Serve over ice if you wish.

TROPICAL DELIGHT

Time to prepare: Approximately ten minutes

Yield: 4 Servings

What You'll Need:

- 1 fresh sprig mint
- 1 tangerine, peeled
- 1/2 mango, peeled and diced
- Filtered water

Procedure:

1. Put in the mint, tangerine, and mango to a glass pitcher. Next, fill it up with filtered water. Let stand minimum 2 hours in a fridge.
2. Pour into serving glasses before you serve.

TROPICAL PARADISE

Time to prepare: Approximately ten minutes

Yield: 4 Servings

What You'll Need:

- 1 kiwi fruit, peeled and cut
- 1 vanilla bean, cut along the length
- 1/2 mango, diced

Procedure:

1. Put in the mango, kiwi and vanilla bean to a 64-ounce pitcher.
2. Put in the filtered water or coconut water.
3. Next, place in your fridge until cold before you serve.

VANILLA AND CARDAMOM ORANGE

Time to prepare: Approximately ten minutes

Yield: 4 Servings

What You'll Need:

- 1 large-sized orange, cut
- 1 tablespoon cardamom
- 1 vanilla bean, cut along the length
- 2-3 cloves

Procedure:

1. Place the ingredients together with filtered water into your pitcher.
2. Put in a fridge and use within a few days.

VANILLA PEACH WATER

Time to prepare: Approximately ten minutes

Yield: 4 Servings

What You'll Need:

- 1 peach, pitted and cubed
- 2 vanilla beans, cut along the length
- Sparkling water

Procedure:

1. Put in the ingredients to a bottle and store in your refrigerator until ready to drink.

2. You must be able to refill your bottle with sparkling water for a few times before you have to replace your ingredients. Happy drinking!

VANILLA PLUM WATER

Time to prepare: Approximately ten minutes

Yield: 2 Servings

What You'll Need:

- 2 cups sparkling water
- 1-2 red plums, cut into chunks
- 1/2 teaspoon vanilla extract
- 2-3 cloves

Procedure:

1. Put plum, cloves, and vanilla into a cocktail shaker. Next, purée them with a muddler.
2. Pour in sparkling water, and let it chill before you serve.

VANILLA STRAWBERRY WATER

Time to prepare: Approximately fifteen minutes

Yield: 4 Servings

What You'll Need:

- 1 cup water
- 2 vanilla beans, cut along the length
- 4 frozen strawberries, hulled and quartered.

Procedure:

1. Mix strawberries in your blender. Move to your bottle. Put in vanilla beans and water. Let stand in your refrigerator.
2. You can put in new water when the bottle is half-way empty.

WATERMELON COCONUT WATER

Time to prepare: **Approximately ten minutes**

Yield: **4 Servings**

What You'll Need:

- 1 medium lime, squeezed
- 1 quart coconut water
- 1/2 small-sized seedless watermelon, cubed

Procedure:

1. Combine the watermelon in a blender. Next, pour the pureed watermelon through the sieve.
2. Pour in coconut water and lime juice.
3. Serve completely chilled over crushed ice.

WINTER RELAXER

Time to prepare: Approximately ten minutes

Yield: 4 Servings

What You'll Need:

- 1 grapefruit, peeled and cut
- 1 tablespoon lavender
- 1 tablespoon mint
- Tea bag

Procedure:

1. Put in all ingredients to a large-sized pitcher. Stir to blend and put in a fridge until serving time.
2. Serve in wine glasses and enjoy!

ICED TEA RECIPES

APPLE AND LEMON ZINGER

Time to prepare: Approximately twenty minutes

Yield: 4 Servings

What You'll Need:

- 1 stick cinnamon
- 2 cups apple juice
- 4 cups boiling water
- 4 lemon zinger tea bags

Procedure:

1. Put tea bags and boiling water in a heat-proof pitcher; allow to steep for approximately twenty minutes.
2. Take away the tea bags, put in apple juice and serve over ice cubes.

BERRYLICIOUS ICED TEA

Time to prepare: Approximately fifteen minutes

Yield: 6 Servings

What You'll Need:

- 1 tablespoon orange juice
- 2 black tea bags
- 3 tablespoons fresh mint leaves
- 4 mixed berry tea bags
- 6 cup water
- Agave syrup, as per taste

Procedure:

1. Bring water to its boiling point. Pour boiled water over tea bags in the pitcher; steep tea bags for approximately ten minutes.
2. Next, discard tea bags. Chill covered for approximately 2 hours.
3. Mix in agave, orange juice, and mint leaves. Serve completely chilled and enjoy!

BLACKBERRY ICED TEA

Time to prepare: Approximately fifteen minutes

Yield: 6 Servings

What You'll Need:

- 1/3 cup honey
- 2 cups frozen blackberries
- 5 cups water
- 5 strawberry tea bags

Procedure:

1. Steep strawberry tea bags in 5 cups of water for eight to ten minutes. Let chill overnight.
2. In a blender, mix 2 cups of frozen blackberries, 1 cup of steeped tea and honey.
3. Put in blackberry puree to the steeped tea, stir, and pour into glasses.

BLUEBERRY AND LAVENDER ICED TEA

Time to prepare: Approximately fifteen minutes

Yield: 6 Servings

What You'll Need:

- 1 tablespoon lemon juice
- 1/2 cup blueberry
- 2 tablespoons dried lavender
- 6 cups boiling water
- 6 tea bags

Procedure:

1. In a pitcher, place a boiling water and tea bags. Allow to stand for a few minutes.
2. Lightly squeeze tea bags and discard them. Put in the remaining ingredients. Enjoy!

CHAMOMILE AND ORANGE ICED TEA

Time to prepare: Approximately 2 hours ten minutes

Yield: 8 Servings

What You'll Need:

- 1/2 grapefruit, cut into wedges
- 1/4 cup chamomile tea
- 3/4 cup orange juice
- 4 cups boiling water

Procedure:

1. Steep chamomile tea in boiling water roughly five minutes.
2. Strain the tea and pour it into a pitcher. Mix in orange juice; sweeten with honey or another natural sweetener.
3. Pour in cold water and place in your fridge until it is chilled or for approximately 2 hours. Serve with grapefruit wedges and enjoy.

CHERRY ICED TEA

Time to prepare: Approximately ten minutes

Yield: 8 Servings

What You'll Need:

- 1/4 cup fresh lemonade
- 2 quarts brewed green tea
- 3 (11.5-ounce) bottles cherry nectar
- Agave nectar, to taste

Procedure:

1. Stir all the above ingredients in your pitchers or bottles. Next, move tea to a fridge.
2. Serve completely chilled and decorated with lemon wedges if you wish.

CHINESE SPEARMINT ICED TEA

Time to prepare: Approximately ten minutes

Yield: 4 Servings

What You'll Need:

- 1 tablespoon loose Chinese green tea
- 1/3 cup honey
- 2 bunches fresh spearmint, washed and drained
- 5 cups boiling water

Procedure:

1. Mix Chinese green tea and 5 cups boiling water in a teapot; steep for two to 4 minutes.

2. Put in spearmint and honey, stirring until well blended. Steep for about four minutes more. Strain your tea and chill until ready to serve; enjoy!

CINNAMON PEAR ICED TEA

Time to prepare: Approximately ten minutes

Yield: 6 Servings

What You'll Need:

- 1 ½ cups unsweetened pear juice
- 1 cinnamon stick
- 1 tablespoon lemon juice
- 2 ½ tablespoons agave nectar
- 2 tablespoons fresh ginger, minced
- 6 black tea bags
- 6 cups water

Procedure:

1. In a deep cooking pan, bring water to its boiling point. Next, turn off burner and put in cinnamon stick and tea bags.
2. Now leave it to steep for five to seven minutes. Next, discard tea bags and put in the rest of ingredients.
3. Chill minimum 2 hours before you serve. Serve completely chilled.

CITRUS AND ROSEMARY ICED TEA

Time to prepare: Approximately fifteen minutes

Yield: 4 Servings

What You'll Need:

- 1 orange, peeled and cut
- 2 green tea bags of your choice
- 2 tablespoons agave nectar
- 3 small sprigs rosemary
- 4 cups boiling water
- Juice of 1 fresh lime

Procedure:

1. Put all the above ingredients in a big pitcher.
2. Stir to blend and serve over ice cubes. Enjoy!

CLASSIC LIME ICED TEA

Time to prepare: Approximately 1 hour ten minutes

Yield: 8 Servings

What You'll Need:

- 1/2 cup lime juice
- 3 orange pekoe tea bags
- 8 cups water

- Honey, to taste

Procedure:

1. In a deep cooking pan, heat 8 cups water to a quick boil. Next, drop in the tea bags and turn off the heat. Now cover and allow to steep minimum 1 hour.
2. In a big glass jar, mix the steeped tea with lime juice and honey. Place in your fridge until chilled and serve over ice if you wish.

GINGER AND MINT ICED TEA

Time to prepare: Approximately fifteen minutes

Yield: 2 Servings

What You'll Need:

- 2 tablespoons agave nectar
- 6 mint tea bags
- 6 ounces fresh ginger root, peeled
- 8 cups boiling water
- Mint sprigs

Procedure:

1. In a teapot, mix ginger, tea bags, and boiling water. Allow to steep for eight to ten minutes.

2. Pour it through a sieve to discard solids. Mix in agave nectar. Let cool in a fridge.
3. Serve over ice decorated with mint sprigs. Enjoy!

GINGER ORANGE ICED TEA

Time to prepare: Approximately ten minutes

Yield: 8 Servings

What You'll Need:

- 1/2 cup honey
- 1/2 lemon, juiced
- 1-inch ginger root, peeled and cut
- 4 orange tea bags
- 4 tea bags
- 6 cups boiling water
- Cold water, as required

Procedure:

1. Put tea bags and boiling water in a large-sized jar; then, steep about half an hour.
2. Take out the tea bags and mix in rest of the ingredients.
3. Finally, let it cool in your fridge. Serve completely chilled over ice and enjoy!

GINGER PINEAPPLE ICED TEA

Time to prepare: Approximately ten minutes

Yield: 4 Servings

What You'll Need:

- 1 cup unsweetened pineapple juice
- 1 tablespoon lime juice
- 2 tablespoons fresh ginger, minced
- 3 tablespoons honey
- 4 cups water
- 4 tea bags

Procedure:

1. In a large-sized deep cooking pan, bring water to its boiling point. Next, turn off burner.
2. Put in the tea bags and leave it to steep roughly five minutes. Next, discard your tea bags; put in the rest of the ingredients.
3. Chill for a few hours before you serve. Enjoy with ice!

HIBISCUS AND POMEGRANATE TEA

Time to prepare: Approximately 2 hours ten minutes

Yield: 8 Servings

What You'll Need:

- 1 cup pomegranate nectar
- 1/4 cup loose hibiscus tea
- 4 cups boiling water
- 4 cups cold water
- Orange wedges, for decoration

Procedure:

1. Steep hibiscus tea in boiling water for about five minutes.
2. Strain the tea, and pour it into a pitcher.
3. Mix in pomegranate nectar and cold water. Place in your fridge until chilled. Serve over ice with orange wedges, if you wish.
4. Store in your fridge for maximum one week. Enjoy!

JASMINE TEA WITH ALMOND MILK

Time to prepare: Approximately twenty minutes

Yield: 8 Servings

What You'll Need:

- 8 jasmine tea bags
- Lime slices, for decoration
- 1/4 cup honey
- 1/4 cup heavy cream
- 1/4 cup unsweetened almond milk

Procedure:

1. Bring 6 cups water to its boiling point and put in the tea bags. Turn off burner and let the tea steep about five minutes.
2. Put in honey, heavy cream, and almond milk. Decorate using lime slices. Finally, place in your fridge until cold. Serve the tea over crushed ice.

LEMONGRASS ICED TEA

Time to prepare: Approximately fifteen minutes

Yield: 2 Servings

What You'll Need:

- 1 cup brewed black tea, cooled
- 1 tablespoon honey
- 2 stalks lemongrass, chopped
- Zest of 1 lemon

Procedure:

1. Put lemongrass and lemon zest into a heatproof pitcher. Pour 2 cups of boiling water over it; allow to steep for fifteen to twenty minutes. Strain and put in honey.
2. Divide prepared liquid among two ice-filled glasses. Top with black tea and serve chilled.

LEMONGRASS ICED TEA

Time to prepare: Approximately ten minutes

Yield: 1 Serving

What You'll Need:

- 1 ½ tablespoons lemongrass juice
- 1 cup iced tea
- 1 stick lemongrass
- 2 lemon slices
- Sugarcane syrup, to taste

Procedure:

1. Put iced tea and lemongrass juice in your mixer; shake thoroughly, and pour into glasses over crushed ice.
2. Put in lemon slices and sweeten with sugarcane syrup.
3. Decorate using 1 stick of lemongrass. Serve completely chilled.

LIME CUCUMBER ICED TEA

Time to prepare: Approximately 2 hours twenty minutes

Yield: 8 Servings

What You'll Need:

- 1/2 cup cucumber, cut

- 1/4 cup wildflower honey
- 2 limes, cut, or as you wish
- 2 quarts boiling water
- 5 tea bags

Procedure:

1. Pour boiling water into a pitcher.
2. Put in the rest of the ingredients.
3. Place in your fridge it for approximately 2 hours or until flavors have infused. Serve completely chilled.

LIMEADE ICED TEA

Time to prepare: Approximately fifteen minutes

Yield: 10 Servings

What You'll Need:

- 1 (6-ounce) can key lime concentrate
- 1 cup mint leaves, loosely packed
- 3 cups simmering water
- 4 cups cold water
- 4 tea bags

Procedure:

1. Pour simmering water into a deep cooking pan. Next, put in tea bags and fresh mint leaves. Cover and steep for approximately ten minutes.
2. Next, discard tea bags and mint leaves. Sweeten with natural sweetener of choice.
3. Put in 4 cups cold water and lime concentrate. Serve over ice cubes.

MANGO GREEN TEA

Time to prepare: Approximately fifteen minutes

Yield: 4 Servings

What You'll Need:

- 1 cup mango nectar
- 1 cup strongly brewed green tea
- 1 sprig sage
- Mango slivers, for decoration

Procedure:

1. Mix tea, sage and mango nectar in a bottle or heat-proof pitcher.
2. Serve over ice decorated with mango slivers.

MAPLE RASPBERRY TEA

Time to prepare: Approximately fifteen minutes

Yield: 10 Servings

What You'll Need:

- 1 cup fresh raspberries
- 1 gallon water
- 1/2 cup powdered lemonade mix
- 2 tablespoons maple syrup
- 3 tea bags

Procedure:

1. In a large-sized deep cooking pan, bring the water to its boiling point. Put in tea bags and raspberries.
2. Let this mixture steep for about five minutes; take out the tea bags; now put in the maple syrup and lemonade mix and stir until completely blended.
3. Let cool in the refrigerator and serve over ice cubes.

MINT AND LAVENDER TEA

Time to prepare: Approximately ten minutes

Yield: 6 Servings

What You'll Need:

- 1/2 cup mint leaves
- 2 tablespoons agave nectar

- 2 tablespoons dried lavender

Procedure:

1. Combine all ingredients. Pour in 4 cups of boiling water.
2. Serve chilled or at room temperature. Enjoy!

MINT CUCUMBER ICED TEA

Time to prepare: Approximately fifteen minutes

Yield: 8 Servings

What You'll Need:

- 1 cucumber, cut
- 1/4 cup honey
- 3 sprigs mint leaves
- 4 green tea bags

Procedure:

1. Bring about 2 cups of water to its boiling point in a moderate-sized pan. Take it off the heat and put in the remaining ingredients.
2. Cover and allow it to sit for about fifteen minutes.
3. Put in honey and stir until the honey is dissolved. Drink completely chilled.

MINT LEMONADE ICED TEA

Time to prepare: Approximately twenty-five minutes

Yield: 12 Servings

What You'll Need:

- 1 (6-ounce) can lemonade concentrate, thawed
- 1 quart boiling water
- 1 tablespoon fresh sage leaves, crushed
- 1/2 cup instant iced tea powder
- 1/4 cup honey
- 2 quarts water
- 3 tablespoons fresh mint leaves, crushed

Procedure:

1. In a pitcher, mix the mint leaves, sage leaves, boiling water, and tea powder. Stir to blend well and allow it to stand for fifteen minutes.
2. Put in the cold water, lemonade concentrate, and honey. Strain out mint and sage leaves and serve your tea over ice.

MOM'S CRANBERRY TEA

Time to prepare: Approximately thirty-five minutes

Yield: 12 Servings

What You'll Need:

- 1 (12- ounce) can cranberry juice concentrate
- 1 gallon water
- 13 tea bags

Procedure:

1. Bring water to its boiling point in a large-sized pot.
2. Now put in tea bags and allow to steep until desired strength is reached. Pour in cranberry juice and stir until blended. Sweeten with agave nectar or the other natural sweetener of choice.
3. Serve thoroughly chilled and enjoy!

ORANGE AND APRICOT ICED TEA

Time to prepare: Approximately ten minutes

Yield: 4 Servings

What You'll Need:

- 1/4 cup fresh orange juice
- 2 quarts brewed tea
- 3 (11.5-ounce) cans apricot nectar
- Agave nectar, to taste

Procedure:

1. Stir all the above ingredients in a pitcher. Next, move prepared tea to a fridge.
2. Serve completely chilled over ice cubes. Decorate using orange wedges.

ORANGE AND LEMON ICED TEA

Time to prepare: Approximately 1 hour ten minutes

Yield: 16 Servings

What You'll Need:

- 1 (12-ounce) can frozen lemonade concentrate
- 1/2 cup honey
- 1/2 lemon, juiced
- 4 green tea bags
- 4 orange tea bags
- 6 cups boiling water
- Cold water, as required

Procedure:

1. Put tea bags in a 1-gallon glass jar. Now pour boiling water over tea bags; then, steep for fifteen to half an hour.
2. Take out the tea bags and mix in lemonade concentrate, lemon juice, and honey.

3. Fill your jar with cold water. Next, let it cool in your fridge. Serve thoroughly chilled and enjoy!

PEACH AND MANGO ICED TEA

Time to prepare: Approximately ten minutes

Yield: 10 Servings

What You'll Need:

- 1 cup mango, chopped
- 12 cups purified water
- 2 peaches, pitted and diced
- 6 white tea bags

Procedure:

1. Bring water to its boiling point. Next, pour boiling water over tea bags. Now turn off burner and leave it to steep for approximately seven minutes.
2. Put in peaches and mango to a big pitcher. Pour in prepared tea and stir until blended and serve.

PEACH ICED TEA

Time to prepare: Approximately 1 hour ten minutes

Yield: 8 Servings

What You'll Need:

- 1 peach, pitted and cut
- 1 tablespoon agave syrup, or to taste
- 1 tangerine, peeled and segmented
- 4 Grey tea bags
- 8 cups boiling water

Procedure:

1. Put peach, tangerine, and agave syrup in a pitcher.
2. Next, purée your fruit using a wooden spoon; put in boiling water and Grey tea bags; stir until blended. Serve completely chilled. Enjoy and stay hydrated!

PEPPERMINT ORANGE TEA

Time to prepare: Approximately forty minutes

Yield: 8 Servings

What You'll Need:

- 1 blood orange, peeled and segmented
- 1 peppermint tea bag
- 1 quart water
- 1/4 cup frozen lemonade concentrate
- 6 tea bags of choice

Procedure:

1. Bring the water to its boiling point in a big pot using high heat; put in orange and tea bags.
2. Next, let it slowly steep for half an hour to an hour. Next, take out the tea bag and mix in the lemonade concentrate. Drink completely chilled.

POMEGRANATE ICED TEA

Time to prepare: **Approximately ten minutes**

Yield: **10 Servings**

What You'll Need:

- 1/2 pomegranate
- 2 tablespoons honey
- 4 cups boiling water
- 6 tea bags

Procedure:

1. Pour boiling water over tea bags in a teapot. Cover and brew for about five minutes.
2. Put in pomegranate and honey and stir until blended.
3. Pour over ice cubes. Enjoy!

RASPBERRY BASIL ICED TEA

Time to prepare: **Approximately twenty minutes**

Yield: 8 Servings

What You'll Need:

- 1 cup fresh basil leaves
- 1 cup water
- 1 pound raspberries
- 1/4 cup agave nectar
- 8 tea bags
- Ice cubes, for serving

Procedure:

1. Bring 6 cups of water to its boiling point in a moderate-sized pan. Turn off burner, put in tea bags, and allow to steep for five to ten minutes.
2. Put raspberries in a container. Bring 1 cup of water to its boiling point. Turn off the heat, and put in agave nectar and basil; allow to steep for ten to twelve minutes.
3. Pour it over raspberries and discard basil leaves. Let cool; put in to prepared tea.
4. Place in your fridge until chilled and serve over ice cubes.

RASPBERRY CHAMOMILE ICED TEA

Time to prepare: Approximately ten minutes

Yield: 6 Servings

What You'll Need:

- 1 pint fresh raspberries
- 1 vanilla bean, cut along the length
- 6 bags chamomile tea
- 6 cups boiling water

Procedure:

1. Put tea bags and vanilla bean into a heat-proof pitcher; put in boiling water and allow it to stand for about five minutes.
2. Take out the tea bags and move your drink to a fridge in order to cool to room temperature.
3. In the meantime, puree raspberries in your blender. Next, sieve them to remove the seeds.
4. Put in the raspberry puree to your tea. Serve completely chilled and enjoy!

RASPBERRY GRAPE ICED TEA

Time to prepare: **Approximately ten minutes**

Yield: **8 Servings**

What You'll Need:

- 1 (16-ounce) bottle orange tender drink, chilled
- 1 cup raspberries
- 1 lime, cut

- 2 family-size tea bags
- 3 cups grape juice
- 4 cups water

Procedure:

1. Process raspberries in your food processor until the desired smoothness is achieved. Pour raspberry puree through a fine strainer into a big container in order to discard raspberry seeds.
2. Bring 4 cups of water to its boiling point in a large-sized deep cooking pan. Turn off the heat and put in tea bags. Next, cover and steep for about five minutes.
3. Discard tea bags. Put in raspberry puree, grape juice, slices of lime, and orange tender drink. Stir to blend. Sweeten with some natural sweetener such as agave nectar, stevia, or honey.
4. Cover and chill overnight. Serve completely chilled.

RASPBERRY HIBISCUS REFRESHER

Time to prepare: Approximately ten minutes

Yield: 8 Servings

What You'll Need:

- 1/2 cups agave nectar
- 2 cups sparkling apple cider, thoroughly chilled

- 4 cups boiling water
- 8 hibiscus tea bags

Procedure:

1. Pour boiling water over tea bags. Cover and steep for about ten minutes. Now discard tea bags.
2. Mix in agave nectar. Now chill until ready to serve. Pour in sparkling cider; serve over ice cubes.

ROCKET MINT ICED TEA

Time to prepare: Approximately ten minutes

Yield: 1 Serving

What You'll Need:

- 1 tablespoon agave syrup
- 1 tablespoon freshly squeezed lime juice
- 1/2 cup brewed green tea, thoroughly chilled
- 4 baby rocket leaves
- 6 mint leaves

Procedure:

1. In a glass, muddle lime juice with rocket leaves, mint leaves, and agave syrup.
2. Next, pour in a chilled tea.
3. Stir and serve completely chilled.

RUSSIAN-STYLE BEVERAGE

Time to prepare: Approximately fifteen minutes

Yield: 20 Servings

What You'll Need:

- 1 teaspoon ground cloves
- 1/4 cup orange-flavored drink mix
- 1/4 cup lemon-flavored instant tea powder
- 1/4 teaspoon ground nutmeg

Procedure:

1. In a large-sized container, mix all the above ingredients. Move to a pitcher
2. Pour simmering water over it. Use 3 teaspoons per serving size. Serve hot or chilled!

SPARKLING APPLE ICED TEA

Time to prepare: Approximately fifteen minutes

Yield: 6 Servings

What You'll Need:

- 1 cup boiling water
- 1/4 cup sparkling water
- 2 green tea bags

- 2-3 mint sprigs
- 3/4 cup apple juice
- Ice cubes

Procedure:

1. Steep tea bags in boiling water about five minutes. Next, take out the tea bags.
2. Put in the rest of ingredients. Serve completely chilled.

SPARKLING APPLE TEA

Time to prepare: Approximately fifteen minutes

Yield: 12 Servings

What You'll Need:

- 1/2 cup honey
- 3 cups fresh apple juice
- 4 cups boiling water
- 4 cups sparkling water
- 4 tea bags
- Apple slices, for decoration

Procedure:

1. Mix boiling water with tea bags. Allow it to steep for a few minutes.

2. Now discard tea bags, put in honey and apple juice; stir until blended and cool it completely.
3. Finally, put in sparkling water. Serve decorated with apple slices. Enjoy!

SPARKLING BLUEBERRY TEA

Time to prepare: Approximately fifteen minutes

Yield: 6 Servings

What You'll Need:

- 1/2 cup agave nectar
- 3 cups blueberry juice
- 4 cups sparkling water
- 6 cups boiling water
- 6 green tea bags

Procedure:

1. Pour boiling water over tea bags. Allow it to steep for five to ten minutes.
2. Next, discard tea bags; put in agave nectar and blueberry juice; stir until blended and move to a fridge in order to cool.
3. Next, put in sparkling water. Serve completely chilled.

SPARKLING CRANBERRY ICED TEA

Time to prepare: Approximately fifteen minutes

Yield: 12 Servings

What You'll Need:

- 4 cups water
- 2 tea bags
- 3 cups fresh cranberry juice
- 4 cups sparkling water
- Orange rind strips, for decoration
- 1/2 cup maple syrup

Procedure:

1. To start, bring 4 cups of water to its boiling point. Put in maple syrup and cook until it is completely dissolved, stirring periodically.
2. Pour maple water over tea bags. Next, allow it to stand covered for about five minutes. Now discard tea bags, put in cranberry juice, and cool it completely.
3. Pour in sparkling water, split among serving glasses, and decorate with orange rind. Enjoy!

STRAWBERRY GREEN TEA

Time to prepare: Approximately ten minutes

Yield: 6 Servings

What You'll Need:

- 1 cup fresh strawberries
- 1/4 cup lemon juice
- 4 bags green tea
- 4 cups boiling water

Procedure:

1. Pour boiling water over tea bags into a heat-proof pitcher; leave for about five minutes.
2. Take out the tea bags; you can sweeten tea to taste. Put in lemon juice and move to a fridge in order to cool to room temperature.
3. Puree strawberries in a food processor or a blender. Next, you should sieve them to remove the strawberry seeds.
4. Finally, put in the strawberry puree to the chilled tea. Keep this tea in your refrigerator until serving time. Enjoy!

STRAWBERRY LEMON ICED TEA

Time to prepare: Approximately twenty minutes

Yield: 10 Servings

What You'll Need:

- 1 cup fresh lemon juice
- 1 cup strawberries
- 1/2 cup agave syrup
- 10 tea bags
- 3 cups sparkling water
- Berries for skewers

Procedure:

1. Bring 10 cups of water to boil. Turn off burner and put in tea bags; now allow to steep completely. Pour tea into a pitcher and let it cool completely.
2. Place the strawberries and lemon juice into your food processor or a blender; purée until the desired smoothness is achieved. Next, strain puréed mixture in order to discard strawberry seeds.
3. Put in strawberry purée to the tea in the pitcher. Mix in agave syrup and sparkling water. Stir to blend well. Decorate using fruit skewers.

STRAWBERRY TANGERINE TEA

Time to prepare: Approximately fifteen minutes

Yield: 8 Servings

What You'll Need:

- 1 can frozen lemonade concentrate

- 2 cups strawberries, hulled and cut
- 3 tangerines, peeled
- 8 black tea bags

Procedure:

1. Pour 8 cups of boiling water over tea bags in a pitcher. Allow it to steep for a few minutes,
2. Puree strawberries and tangerine in your blender until the mixture is smooth. Put in this pureed mixture to the steeped tea.
3. Put in lemonade concentrate and stir until blended. Enjoy with ice!

SUMMER ORANGE TEA

Time to prepare: Approximately 3 hours 30 minutes

Yield: 4 Servings

What You'll Need:

- 1/4 cup dried chrysanthemums
- 3 orange slices
- 4 cups boiling water
- Agave syrup, to taste

Procedure:

1. Put chrysanthemums and orange slices in a ceramic pot. Pour in boiling water and cover with a lid. Next, allow to steep for five minutes. Mix in agave syrup.
2. Place in your fridge until cold and serve completely chilled or over ice.

TANGERINE AND LAVENDER ICED TEA

Time to prepare: Approximately fifteen minutes

Yield: 12 Servings

What You'll Need:

- 1 ½ teaspoons dried lavender
- 1 tangerine, peeled and cut
- 2 quarts water
- 8 tea bags
- Honey to taste

Procedure:

1. Bring water to its boiling point. Put in tea bags and steep for five minutes; strain tea into a heat-proof pitcher.
2. Put in the rest of the ingredients.
3. Cool thoroughly and serve over crushed ice.

TANGERINE STRAWBERRY ICED TEA

Time to prepare: Approximately fifteen minutes

Yield: 6 Servings

What You'll Need:

- 1 cup pomegranate juice
- 4 strawberry herbal tea bags
- 6 cups water
- 6 tangerine herbal tea bags
- Ice cubes
- Strawberries, for decoration

Procedure:

1. Pour water into a medium-large stock pot. Next, bring water to its boiling point. Put in the tea bags and allow it to sit for about half an hour. Discard tea bags.
2. Now move tea to the big pitcher. Put in pomegranate juice and stir until blended. Finally, sweeten your tea as you wish. Serve decorated with strawberries and ice cubes.

TEA WITH COCONUT MILK

Time to prepare: Approximately twenty minutes

Yield: 4 Servings

What You'll Need:

- 1/4 teaspoon grated nutmeg
- 3/4 cup full-fat coconut milk
- 4 cups simmering water
- 4 tea bags
- Maple syrup, to taste

Procedure:

1. Put 1 tea bag in each mug. Pour simmering water over your tea bag; allow it to steep for about five minutes. Allow to cool to room temperature. Mix in maple syrup.
2. In the meantime, froth coconut milk using a hand blender.
3. Next, gently pour frothed milk over the tea. Drizzle with grated nutmeg before you serve.

TROPICAL ICED TEA

Time to prepare: **Approximately twenty minutes**

Yield: 12 Servings

What You'll Need:

- 1 cup fresh orange juice
- 1 cup pineapple
- 1/2 cup agave syrup
- 12 cups boiling water
- 12 tea bags

- 3 cups lemon soda

Procedure:

1. Put boiling water and tea bags in a teapot; now allow it to steep. Put in a fridge until it is completely chilled.
2. Place the pineapple and orange juice into your blender; purée until the mixture is uniform and smooth. Put in pineapple purée to the pitcher.
3. Finally, put in agave syrup and lemon soda. Stir and serve completely chilled.

VANILLA AND JASMINE TEA

Time to prepare: Approximately 2 hours ten minutes

Yield: 8 Servings

What You'll Need:

- 1 vanilla bean, cut along the length
- 1/2 cup orange juice
- 1/3 cup honey
- 12 green jasmine tea bags
- 4 cups cold water
- 4 cups simmering water

Procedure:

1. Put tea bags and vanilla bean in simmering water for two to three minutes.
2. Take out the tea bags and pour your tea into a big pitcher.
3. Mix in orange juice and honey; stir thoroughly or until the honey is dissolved. Put in 4 cups of cold water. Serve completely chilled and enjoy!

JUICE RECIPES

ANTI-INFLAMMATORY BOOSTER

Time to prepare: **Approximately ten minutes**

Yield: **2 Servings**

What You'll Need:

- 1 orange
- 1 lime
- 1 small handful cilantro
- 2/3 medium pineapple

Procedure:

1. Take the rind off orange and pineapple. Cut them into big wedges; then, move them to a juice extractor. Put in lime and cilantro.
2. Process the ingredients in a juice extractor.
3. Finally, pour prepared juice over ice cubes in glasses. Serve immediately.

APPLE LEMONADE

Time to prepare: **Approximately ten minutes**

Yield: 2 Servings

What You'll Need:

- 1 handful spinach
- 1 lemon, peeled
- 1 small-sized green apple
- 1/2 cucumber
- 1/2 teaspoon allspice

Procedure:

1. Push all of the above ingredients through the juicer.
2. Serve the lemonade over ice and enjoy!

APPLE PIE JUICE

Time to prepare: Approximately ten minutes

Yield: 2 Servings

What You'll Need:

- 1 sweet potato
- 1/4 teaspoon pumpkin pie spice
- 2 apples
- 2 carrots
- 2 oranges

Procedure:

1. Core the apples. Take the rind off sweet potato and oranges. Trim the carrots. Put in them to your juice extractor together with pumpkin pie spices.
2. Juice all the ingredients and pour your juice into a couple of glasses.

APPLE PUMPKIN JUICE

Time to prepare: Approximately ten minutes

Yield: 2 Servings

What You'll Need:

- 1 ½ cups mixed berries
- 1 teaspoon cinnamon powder
- 1/4 teaspoon grated nutmeg
- 2 cups pumpkin
- 2 moderate-sized apples

Procedure:

1. Juice apples, berries, and pumpkin.
2. Next, drizzle with cinnamon powder and nutmeg. Pour the juice into a couple of glasses and serve instantly.

APPLE-ORANGE JUICE

Time to prepare: Approximately ten minutes

Yield: 2 Servings

What You'll Need:

- 1 Granny Smith apple, quartered
- 1 lime, peeled
- 1/2 teaspoon cinnamon, ground
- 1/4 teaspoon ground cloves
- 2 oranges, peeled

Procedure:

1. Process lime, oranges, and apple through a juicer in accordance with manufacturer's directions.
2. Put in cinnamon and cloves and pour into a couple of glasses.

APPLE-SPROUT TREAT

Time to prepare: Approximately ten minutes

Yield: 2 Servings

What You'll Need:

- 1 apple, cored
- 1 cup broccoli sprouts
- 1 lemon, peeled
- 1/2 cup alfalfa sprouts
- 2 medium carrots, trimmed

Procedure:

1. Combine the juice meticulously in your juicer.
2. Pour into a couple of glasses and drink at once.

ARTICHOKE-CARROT BLEND

Time to prepare: Approximately ten minutes

Yield: 2 Servings

What You'll Need:

- 1 bunch fresh cilantro
- 1 celery stalk, chopped
- 1 handful baby spinach
- 3 medium carrots, trimmed
- 4 big radishes, tailed and trimmed
- 4 Jerusalem artichokes

Procedure:

1. Process the artichokes, one by one, through your electronic juicer.
2. Do not forget to roll the spinach and cilantro into a ball to compress while putting in them to a juicer.
3. Put in all the ingredients and juice them.

ASPARAGUS AND TOMATO JUICE

Time to prepare: **Approximately ten minutes**

Yield: **1 Serving**

What You'll Need:

- 1 cucumber
- 1 large-sized tomato
- 1 orange, peeled
- 1 stalk asparagus
- 1/2 teaspoon ground allspice

Procedure:

1. To start, wash your ingredients meticulously. Process the asparagus and tomato through your juicer in accordance with the manufacturer's directions.
2. Put in the remaining ingredients.
3. Combine the juice until everything is well blended; serve over crushed ice.

AUTUMN FLIGHT

Time to prepare: **Approximately fifteen minutes**

Yield: **2 Servings**

What You'll Need:

- 1/2 ground allspice
- 2 carrots

- 2 pears
- 2" ginger root, peeled
- 4 parsnips

Procedure:

1. Wash the ingredients and move them to a juicer.
2. Push the ingredients through the juicer in accordance with manufacturer's instructions.
3. Pour the juice into a couple of glasses. Serve with straws and enjoy!

AUTUMN TREAT

Time to prepare: **Approximately ten minutes**

Yield: **2 Servings**

What You'll Need:

- 1 green bell pepper
- 1 handful cilantro
- 1 small head cauliflower
- 1 sweet potato
- 2 carrots
- 2 Fuji apples

Procedure:

1. Juice the ingredients and pour it into thoroughly chilled serving glasses.

AVOCADO AND APPLE JUICE

Time to prepare: Approximately ten minutes

Yield: 4 Servings

What You'll Need:

- 1 avocado, pitted
- 1 medium cucumber
- 1-inch piece of ginger
- 4 Granny Smith apples, cored

Procedure:

1. Process all the ingredients, apart from for avocado. Next, blend the juice and avocado well.
2. Pour into serving glasses before you serve.

BEET AND PLUM JUICE

Time to prepare: Approximately ten minutes

Yield: 2 Servings

What You'll Need:

- 2 beets

- 2 carrots
- 7 leaves kale Tuscan cabbage
- 8 medium plums

Procedure:

1. Peel your beets and scrub the carrots.
2. Push all of the above ingredients through the juicer.
3. Serve over crushed ice if you wish.

BEET BLAST

Time to prepare: Approximately ten minutes

Yield: 1 Serving

What You'll Need:

- 1 carrot
- 1 orange, peeled
- 2 apples, cored
- 2 celery ribs
- 2 sugar beets

Procedure:

1. Scrub and trim the carrots and the beets. Next, cut them into chunks.
2. After this, process them through the feed tube of your juicer.

3. Put in apples, orange, and the celery. Combine the juice and serve as soon as you can.

BEETROOT, CARROT AND LIME JUICE

Time to prepare: Approximately ten minutes

Yield: 2 Servings

What You'll Need:

- 1 celery
- 1 small-sized lime
- 2 tablespoons of brewer's yeast
- 3 carrots
- 3 moderate-sized beetroot

Procedure:

1. Scrub beetroot, carrots, and celery. Peel the lime, and put in the ingredients to the juicer.
2. Put in brewer's yeast and juice until everything is thoroughly combined. Enjoy!!

BERRY AND APPLE COOLER

Time to prepare: Approximately ten minutes

Yield: 4 Servings

What You'll Need:

- 1 cup blueberries
- 1/2 cup blackberries
- 2 cups strawberries, hulled
- 4 apples, cored

Procedure:

1. Juice the apples through a juicer following manufacturer's directions.
2. Put in the strawberries, followed by the blackberries and the blueberries. Serve over crushed ice.

BERRY AND CARROT COCKTAIL DRINK

Time to prepare: Approximately ten minutes

Yield: 2 Servings

What You'll Need:

- 3/4 cup blueberries
- 3 moderate-sized carrots, trimmed
- 2 pears, cored
- 1/2 cup strawberries

Procedure:

1. Process the blueberries and strawberries through a juicer in accordance with the manufacturer's directions.

2. Put in the carrots and the pears. After this, mix the juice meticulously.

BERRY GRAPEFRUIT MIX

Time to prepare: Approximately ten minutes

Yield: 2 Servings

What You'll Need:

- 1 cup mixed berries
- 1 pink grapefruit, peeled
- 2 oranges, peeled

Procedure:

1. Process the ingredients through the feed tube of a juicer.

BLACK CURRANT AND SPROUT JUICE

Time to prepare: Approximately ten minutes

Yield: 2 Servings

What You'll Need:

- 1 cup red grapes
- 1/2 cup coconut water
- 1/2 cup black currants

- 2 tablespoons alfalfa sprouts

Procedure:

1. Juice the ingredients using a juice machine.
2. You can make the juice sweeter with your favorite natural sweetener if you wish.

BLACKBERRY LEMONADE

Time to prepare: Approximately fifteen minutes

Yield: 2 Servings

What You'll Need:

- 1 (6-ounce) can lemonade concentrate, undiluted
- 1 cup fresh blackberries
- 3 cups cold water

Procedure:

1. Mix blackberries and 1 cup of cold water in your blender until the desired smoothness is achieved.
2. Strain mixed mixture through a sieve. Mix blackberry liquid with the rest of the 2 cups of water and lemonade concentrate. Serve chilled and decorated with mint leaves if you wish.

BLOODY MARY JUICE

Time to prepare: **Approximately ten minutes**

Yield: **4 Servings**

What You'll Need:

- 1 carrot
- 1 small handful basil
- 1 small handful parsley
- 1 teaspoon olive oil
- 2 red bell peppers
- 2 ribs celery
- 4 tomatoes
- A pinch of salt

Procedure:

1. Push all of the above ingredients through the juicer.
2. Pour into four chilled glasses. Serve immediately.

BOK CHOY AND CARROT JUICE

Time to prepare: **Approximately ten minutes**

Yield: **4 Servings**

What You'll Need:

- 1-inch ginger root

- 2 apples, cored
- 2 Bok choy bulbs
- 2 celery ribs
- 4 cabbage leaves
- 6 carrots, trimmed

Procedure:

1. Rinse all ingredients; cut up the ingredients to sizes that fit a juicer.
2. Juice it and serve immediately!

BROCCOLI AND SPROUT JUICE

Time to prepare: Approximately ten minutes

Yield: 2 Servings

What You'll Need:

- 1 crown broccoli, broken into florets
- 1 green apple
- 1 lemon, peeled
- 1 tablespoon alfalfa sprouts
- 2 carrots, trimmed

Procedure:

1. Push all the above ingredients through your juice extractor.

2. Serve over ice in your punch container if you wish.

BRUSSELS SPROUTS JUICE

Time to prepare: Approximately ten minutes

Yield: 2 Servings

What You'll Need:

- 1 ½ cups chopped Brussels sprouts
- 1 head lettuce
- 1 lime
- 1 orange, peeled
- 4 large-sized strawberries

Procedure:

1. Push the ingredients using a juice extractor.
2. Serve in tall thoroughly chilled glasses.

CABBAGE AND BROCCOLI JUICE

Time to prepare: Approximately ten minutes

Yield: 2 Servings

What You'll Need:

- 1 small-sized head broccoli, broken into florets
- 1 small-sized head red cabbage

- 1/2 teaspoon Maca powder
- 3 big leaves Swiss chard, torn into pieces

Procedure:

1. Process the cabbage and broccoli through a juicer.
2. Put in the rest of the ingredients to your juicer.
3. Combine the juice meticulously. Finally, serve the juice over crushed ice if you wish.

CABBAGE AND ORANGE JUICE

Time to prepare: Approximately ten minutes

Yield: 2 Servings

What You'll Need:

- 1 green apple
- 1 orange
- 1 teaspoon Spirulina powder
- 4 leaves red cabbage

Procedure:

1. Core green apple and peel the orange. Move them to a juicer together with cabbage and Spirulina powder.
2. Juice and serve immediately.

CABBAGE APPLE CRUSH

Time to prepare: **Approximately ten minutes**

Yield: 2 Servings

What You'll Need:

- 1 lemon, peeled
- 1 medium apple, cored
- 1 stalk celery with leaves
- 1/2 cup parsley
- 1/2-inch piece ginger
- 1/4 head green cabbage
- 10 collard leaves

Procedure:

1. Process the celery, cabbage and apple through a juicer in accordance with the manufacturer's directions.
2. Put in the remaining ingredients. Serve over ice.

CABBAGE CRUSH

Time to prepare: **Approximately ten minutes**

Yield: 1 Serving

What You'll Need:

- 1 green apple, cored

- 1 ripe pear, cored
- 1/4 green cabbage, cut into wedges
- 1-inch piece of ginger
- 4 sprigs fresh mint
- 6 lettuce leaves

Procedure:

1. Ready all the ingredients before juicing them.
2. Juice all ingredients meticulously. Pour into two chilled glasses and drink as soon as you can.

CABBAGE JUICE WITH RED GRAPES

Time to prepare: Approximately ten minutes

Yield: 2 Servings

What You'll Need:

- 1 apple
- 1 beet
- 1 bunch red grapes
- 4 cabbage leaves

Procedure:

1. Juice the ingredients meticulously.
2. Pour into thoroughly chilled serving glasses.

CANTALOUPE AND BLACKBERRY JUICE

Time to prepare: **Approximately ten minutes**

Yield: **2 Servings**

What You'll Need:

- 1 cup blackberries
- 1/2 cantaloupe, peeled and seeded
- 1/4 cup fresh mint leaves
- 1/4 cup parsley

Procedure:

1. Juice all ingredients meticulously. Pour into two thoroughly chilled glasses.
2. Drink immediately.

CARROT AND MACA LIMEADE

Time to prepare: **Approximately ten minutes**

Yield: **2 Servings**

What You'll Need:

- 1 apple, cored
- 1 lime, peeled and seeded
- 1 pear, cored
- 1 teaspoon Maca powder

- 2 carrots, trimmed

Procedure:

1. Process the ingredients through your electronic juicer in accordance with the manufacturer's directions.
2. Whisk your juice in order to blend well and enjoy right now.

CARROT AND TANGERINE JUICE

Time to prepare: Approximately ten minutes

Yield: 2 Servings

What You'll Need:

- 1 apple, cored
- 1 pear, cored
- 1-inch piece fresh ginger
- 2 carrots, trimmed
- 3 tangerines, peeled

Procedure:

1. Process the carrots, apple, and pear through a juicer.
2. Put in the tangerines, a few pieces at a time. Mix in the ginger and mix the juice meticulously.
3. Enjoy!!

CARROT-FENNEL TREAT

Time to prepare: **Approximately ten minutes**

Yield: 2 Servings

What You'll Need:

- 1 carrot
- 1 fennel
- 1 pear
- 1 small-sized handful parsley
- 2 oranges

Procedure:

1. Blend carrot, fennel, pear, oranges, and parsley together until a smooth juice is achieved.
2. Pour juice into a couple of glasses. Decorate them with orange slices if you wish. Enjoy!

CELERY BLAST

Time to prepare: **Approximately ten minutes**

Yield: 2 Servings

What You'll Need:

- 1/2 teaspoon ground cloves
- 2 pears

- 3 celery roots

Procedure:

1. Rinse all ingredients meticulously. Peel celery and move to a juicer. Put in pear and ground cloves.
2. Push your ingredients through a juicer and serve immediately!

CHARD AND AVOCADO BLEND

Time to prepare: Approximately ten minutes

Yield: 2 Servings

What You'll Need:

- 1 mango, cut into chunks
- 1/2 avocado, pitted and diced
- 1/2 cup coconut water
- 2 leaves Swiss chard, torn into pieces

Procedure:

1. Process Swiss chard and avocado through a juicer.
2. Move it to a blender; put in the mango and coconut water. Blend until the mixture is smooth.
3. Pour the juice into glasses before you serve.

CHAYOTE TOMATO BOOSTER

Time to prepare: **Approximately ten minutes**

Yield: 1 Serving

What You'll Need:

- 1 green apple
- 1 tomato
- 1/2 chayote

Procedure:

1. Rinse all the above ingredients meticulously and put them into the juice extractor.
2. Process all ingredients using the juice extractor. Serve in a big jug and drink instantly.

CHERRY-SWEET POTATO DELIGHT

Time to prepare: **Approximately ten minutes**

Yield: 4 Servings

What You'll Need:

- 1 fennel
- 1 sweet potato
- 1" ginger
- 1/2 cup dried cherries

- 4 tangerines, peeled
- A dash of ground nutmeg

Procedure:

1. Put all of the above ingredients using a juice extractor. Process until you get the juice.
2. Pour the juice into four chilled glasses and decorate with drinking straws.
3. Drizzle with some extra ground nutmeg. Enjoy!

CHILI PEPPER AND SWEET POTATO JUICE

Time to prepare: **Approximately ten minutes**

Yield: 2 Servings

What You'll Need:

- 1 beet, peeled
- 1 chili pepper
- 1 sweet potato, peeled
- 2 oranges, peeled
- 4 carrots

Procedure:

1. Juice the ingredients using a juice machine.
2. The juice is best served over a few ice cubes.

CLEAN & GREEN JUICE

Time to prepare: **Approximately ten minutes**

Yield: 2 Servings

What You'll Need:

- 1 orange, peeled
- 1 pear, cored
- 1/2 small-sized head green cabbage
- 1-inch ginger, peeled
- 6 leaves lettuce

Procedure:

1. Push all of the above ingredients through the juicer.
2. Serve immediately.

COCONUT APPLE PIE

Time to prepare: **Approximately ten minutes**

Yield: 2 Servings

What You'll Need:

- 1 cup coconut water
- 1/4 grated nutmeg
- 2 apples
- 2 cups spinach

- Coconut flakes, for decoration

Procedure:

1. Juice the spinach, apples, and coconut water until everything is blended.
2. Put in an extra water as required. Drizzle with nutmeg and coconut flakes.

COOLING LIMEADE

Time to prepare: Approximately ten minutes

Yield: 2 Servings

What You'll Need:

- 1 lime
- 1/2 moderate-sized honeydew
- 1/2 moderate-sized watermelon
- 1/2 cup fresh mint

Procedure:

1. Take the rind off honeydew and watermelon.
2. Rinse all ingredients meticulously and move them to a juice extractor.
3. Juice all the above ingredients and serve instantly.

CRANBERRY TREAT

Time to prepare: **Approximately ten minutes**

Yield: 2 Servings

What You'll Need:

- 1 cup cranberries
- 1/2 cup fresh pineapple chunks
- 2 carrots, trimmed

Procedure:

1. Process the cranberries, carrots, and pineapple according to the manufacturer's instructions.
2. Put in crushed ice if you wish. Serve as soon as you can and enjoy.

CUCUMBER AND CARROT COCKTAIL

Time to prepare: **Approximately ten minutes**

Yield: 2 Servings

What You'll Need:

- 1 apple, cored
- 1 carrot
- 1 cucumber
- 1/2 head lettuce

- Water to make 1 cup juice

Procedure:

1. Juice the ingredients and serve over ice cubes.

CUCUMBER AND CARROT JUICE

Time to prepare: Approximately ten minutes

Yield: 2 Servings

What You'll Need:

- 1 celery rib
- 1 cucumber
- 1 handful parsley
- 1 lime, peeled
- 1" ginger, peeled
- 2 carrots

Procedure:

1. Rinse all ingredients and press them through your juicer.
2. Serve in thoroughly chilled glasses.

CUCUMBER ORANGE DELIGHT

Time to prepare: Approximately ten minutes

Yield: 1 Serving

What You'll Need:

- 1 bunch of parsley
- 1 cucumber
- 1 green apple
- 1 lime
- 1 orange

Procedure:

1. Rinse all the above ingredients well; then, put them through a juice extractor.

DAILY GARDEN JUICE

Time to prepare: Approximately ten minutes

Yield: 2 Servings

What You'll Need:

- 1 apple
- 1 stalk broccoli
- 1/2 yellow squash
- 2 leaves Tuscan cabbage
- 3 carrots

Procedure:

1. Rinse all the above ingredients meticulously.

2. Push juice ingredients through a juicer. Pour into two glasses and serve immediately!

FAVORITE BROCCOLI BREAKFAST

Time to prepare: Approximately ten minutes

Yield: 2 Servings

What You'll Need:

- 1 celery rib
- 1 small-sized lemon with peel
- 1-inch young ginger root
- 2 green apples, cored
- 3 branches broccoli
- 6 leaves Iceberg lettuce

Procedure:

1. Rinse the ingredients meticulously.
2. Cut up the ingredients to sizes that fit your juicer. Next, juice them and serve your juice in a couple of glasses.

FENNEL PURPLE JUICE

Time to prepare: Approximately ten minutes

Yield: 2 Servings

What You'll Need:

- 1 fennel
- 1 tablespoon fresh parsley
- 2 beets beetroot, peeled
- 1 orange, peeled
- 1/2 cup baby spinach

Procedure:

1. Rinse all ingredients meticulously and move them to a juicer.
2. Put in the ingredients through juicer and serve!

FIT RED TREAT

Time to prepare: Approximately ten minutes

Yield: 2 Servings

What You'll Need:

- 1 ½" ginger, peeled
- 1 beetroot, peeled
- 1 sweet potato, peeled
- 2 apples, cored

Procedure:

1. Rinse all ingredients and add them to your juice extractor.

2. Process all the above ingredients through a juicer and serve immediately.

FRESH MORNING DRINK

Time to prepare: Approximately ten minutes

Yield: 2 Servings

What You'll Need:

- 1 tomato
- 1 beet
- 1 small handful basil
- 1/2 cup cherries, pitted
- 1/4 medium watermelon

Procedure:

1. Take the rind off watermelon and peel the beet. Put in it to the juicer together with rest of the ingredients.
2. Juice the ingredients using a juice machine. Sweeten with natural sweetener if you wish.

FRUIT AND CILANTRO JUICE

Time to prepare: Approximately ten minutes

Yield: 2 Servings

What You'll Need:

- 1 bunch fresh cilantro
- 1 lime, peeled
- 1 pear, cored
- 1 teaspoon Spirulina powder
- 2 Granny Smith apples, cored
- 4 stalks celery, chopped

Procedure:

1. Juice celery, apples, pear, cilantro, lime, and spirulina in your electric juicer.
2. Split the juice between two tall thoroughly chilled glasses; serve immediately.

FRUITY DETOX

Time to prepare: Approximately ten minutes

Yield: 1 Serving

What You'll Need:

- 1 mango
- 1 jalapeño
- 1 lemon
- 1/2 cucumber
- 1/2 yellow pepper

Procedure:

1. Push the ingredients in your juicer.
2. Enjoy with ice!

FRUITY HERBY DELIGHT

Time to prepare: Approximately ten minutes

Yield: 3 Servings

What You'll Need:

- 1 apple
- 1 pear
- 1 tablespoon fresh basil
- 1 tablespoon fresh parsley
- 1" ginger
- 1/2 small-sized pineapple
- 2 grapefruits

Procedure:

1. Start by cleaning and preparing your ingredients. Now move them to a juice extractor.
2. Push the mixture through juice extractor.

GARDEN GOLD

Time to prepare: Approximately fifteen minutes

Yield: 4 Servings

What You'll Need:

- 1 bell pepper, seeded
- 1 cucumber
- 2 cups purple cabbage
- 2 heads lettuce
- 2 red tomatoes

Procedure:

1. Juice the ingredients and serve in thoroughly chilled glasses.
2. If you desire to get rid of acne, drink this juice every day.

GINGER KALE JUICE

Time to prepare: Approximately ten minutes

Yield: 2 Servings

What You'll Need:

- 1 cucumber
- 1 small-sized lemon, peeled
- 1/2 head red lettuce
- 1-inch piece fresh ginger
- 6 leaves kale

Procedure:

1. Process the ingredients through a juicer in accordance with the manufacturer's directions.
2. Pour into glasses before you serve.

GINGER-PEAR DELIGHT

Time to prepare: **Approximately ten minutes**

Yield: **2 Servings**

What You'll Need:

- 1 handful kale
- 1 pear
- 1-inch ginger
- 2 celery roots
- 2 sprigs rosemary

Procedure:

1. Rinse and clean all of the above ingredients. Move them to a juicer.
2. Juice the ingredients and pour it into the glasses. Serve immediately.

GRAPE AND PEAR JUICE

Time to prepare: **Approximately ten minutes**

Yield: **2 Servings**

What You'll Need:

- 1 crown broccoli
- 1 cup green grapes
- 2 handfuls spinach
- 2 pears

Procedure:

1. Juice the ingredients and serve immediately.
2. Decorate the juice with frozen grapes if you wish.

GRAPE AND SUGAR BEETS

Time to prepare: Approximately ten minutes

Yield: 2 Servings

What You'll Need:

- 1 medium carrot, trimmed
- 1/2 pound black grapes, seedless
- 2 sugar beets, with greens

Procedure:

1. Trim the beets and after that cut them into pieces. Move the beets to your electronic juicer; process them in accordance with the manufacturer's instructions.
2. Put in the carrots and black grapes.
3. Whisk the juice before you serve. Try to drink instantly.

GRAPE POMEADE

Time to prepare: Approximately ten minutes

Yield: 2 Servings

What You'll Need:

- 1 cup fresh pomegranate juice
- 1 lime, peeled
- 2 cups red grapes
- 4 leaves beet greens

Procedure:

1. Juice the ingredients and move to the serving glasses.

GRAPEFRUIT AND CRANBERRY DELIGHT

Time to prepare: Approximately ten minutes

Yield: 2 Servings

What You'll Need:

- 1 cup cranberries
- 1 grapefruit, peeled
- 1 pear, cored
- 1 sweet potato, peeled
- 5 leaves collard greens

Procedure:

1. Process everything through a juicer in accordance with the manufacturer's directions.
2. Fill serving glasses with ice cubes; pour the juice into the glasses. Serve immediately.

GRAPEFRUIT MINT JUICE

Time to prepare: Approximately ten minutes

Yield: 2 Servings

What You'll Need:

- 1 grapefruit
- 1 lime
- 1 small handful mint
- 1/2 fennel
- 3 carrots
- 5 leaves kale

Procedure:

1. Scrub the carrots, and peel your grapefruit and lime.
2. Next, rinse all the ingredients meticulously and move them to a juicer together with the rest of ingredients.
3. Process the ingredients and serve.

GRAPEFRUIT-FENNEL DELIGHT

Time to prepare: Approximately ten minutes

Yield: 2 Servings

What You'll Need:

- 1 grapefruit
- 1 lime
- 1 orange
- 1 small handful mint
- 1/2 fennel
- 2 celery ribs
- 5 leaves Tuscan cabbage

Procedure:

1. Push all of the above ingredients through the juicer.
2. Enjoy!

GRAPE-MELON BLAST

Time to prepare: Approximately ten minutes

Yield: 3 Servings

What You'll Need:

- 1 cup green grapes, seedless
- 1 lemon, peeled

- 1/4 small honeydew melon
- 2 kiwi fruits, peeled
- 3/4 cup spinach, torn into pieces

Procedure:

1. Combine the juice meticulously to blend all the above ingredients.
2. Serve immediately and enjoy!

GREEN & YUM

Time to prepare: Approximately fifteen minutes

Yield: 2 Servings

What You'll Need:

- 1 kiwi, peeled
- 1 peach, pitted
- 2 apples
- 2 cups chopped mustard greens
- 2 stalks celery

Procedure:

1. Push the ingredients in your juicer.
2. Pour into glasses and serve immediately.

GREEN BLAST

Time to prepare: Approximately ten minutes

Yield: 2 Servings

What You'll Need:

- 1 cucumber
- 1 small-sized pear
- 1/4 small-sized honeydew melon
- 4 leaves kale

Procedure:

1. Start by removing rind from honeydew melon. Then put the melon in your juicer.
2. Put in the pear, kale, and cucumber. Now push all ingredients through your juicer and serve in a tall glass.
3. Decorate using melon balls if you wish. Enjoy!

GREEN CLEANSER

Time to prepare: Approximately ten minutes

Yield: 2 Servings

What You'll Need:

- 1 ½ cups arugula
- 1 lime

- 1 medium apple
- 1/2-inch slice of fresh ginger
- 2 cups spinach

Procedure:

1. Rinse and wash the spinach and arugula. Next, tear them into pieces. Core the apple, and take the rind off the lime.
2. Juice all the ingredients; serve the juice chilled.

GREEN FANATIC

Time to prepare: Approximately fifteen minutes

Yield: 4 Servings

What You'll Need:

- 1 ½ cups strawberries
- 1 lime
- 2 apples
- 4 cups watermelon
- 6 leaves collards

Procedure:

1. Hull strawberries and torn collard leaves. Take the rind off watermelon. Core your apples and peel the lime.

2. Put all the ingredients using a juice extractor. Juice and serve thoroughly chilled.

GREEN FOREST

Time to prepare: Approximately ten minutes

Yield: 2 Servings

What You'll Need:

- 1 carrot
- 1 cucumber
- 1 cup broccoli
- 1 green apple
- 1 lime
- 1 stalk celery

Procedure:

1. Process all ingredients in your juice extractor.
2. Pour into two thoroughly chilled tall glasses.

GREEN JUICE WITH DATES

Time to prepare: Approximately ten minutes

Yield: 2 Servings

What You'll Need:

- 1 cup strawberries
- 1 small-sized anise bulb
- 4 dates
- 4 handfuls spinach

Procedure:

1. Juice anise bulb and spinach. Move the mixture to a blender together with dates and strawberries.
2. Blend to blend. Serve over ice cubes and enjoy.

GREEN PEAR JUICE

Time to prepare: Approximately ten minutes

Yield: 2 Servings

What You'll Need:

- 1 bunch cilantro
- 1 cucumber
- 1 cup spinach
- 1 pear
- 2 carrots
- 3 leaves kale

Procedure:

1. Juice all the above ingredients together and serve.

GREEN ROCKET JUICE

Time to prepare: **Approximately ten minutes**

Yield: 2 Servings

What You'll Need:

- 1 apple
- 1 handful fresh cilantro
- 1 pear
- 2 cups coconut water
- 2 handfuls kale

Procedure:

1. Tear kale and cilantro into pieces, cored the apple and pear. Move them to a juicer together with coconut water.
2. Juice everything, pour into two thoroughly chilled glasses and serve immediately.
3. This juice is great for our skin, hair, and nails.

GREEN SOY COCONUT JUICE

Time to prepare: **Approximately ten minutes**

Yield: 2 Servings

What You'll Need:

- 2 apples
- 2 cups coconut water
- 2 handfuls baby spinach
- 2 handfuls of arugula
- Soy sauce, to taste

Procedure:

1. Rinse the ingredients meticulously. Juice spinach, arugula, and apples.
2. Mix the mixture with coconut water and soy sauce. Serve immediately.
3. The juice provides you with significant digestive tract benefits. Not recommended for those with a soy allergy. Enjoy!

HERB AND LIME JUICE

Time to prepare: **Approximately ten minutes**

Yield: 2 Servings

What You'll Need:

- 1 big cucumber
- 1 handful cilantro
- 1 handful mint
- 1 lime
- 2 handfuls spinach

Procedure:

1. Juice the ingredients and serve it immediately.

HERBY ENERGY DRINK

Time to prepare: Approximately ten minutes

Yield: 2 Servings

What You'll Need:

- 1 handful fresh basil
- 1 lemon, peeled
- 2 beetroots, peeled
- 2 carrots
- 2 oranges, peeled

Procedure:

1. Push all of the above ingredients through the juicer and serve instantly.

HOT BEET JUICE

Time to prepare: Approximately ten minutes

Yield: 4 Servings

What You'll Need:

- 1 beet
- 1 teaspoon salt
- 1/2 cup kale
- 2 red bell peppers, seeded
- 3 celery stalks
- 3 tomatoes
- 4 carrots, trimmed
- 4 green onions, trimmed
- A few drops hot pepper sauce
- A pinch of black pepper

Procedure:

1. Rinse all the ingredients.
2. Process the carrots, celery and beet through your electronic juicer according to the manufacturer's instructions.
3. Put in the kale, followed by tomatoes, bell peppers, and green onions. Sprinkle with salt, black pepper, and hot sauce.
4. Finally, whisk the juice meticulously, and serve over ice. Enjoy!

HOT SWISS CHARD JUICE

Time to prepare: Approximately ten minutes

Yield: 2 Servings

What You'll Need:

- 1 bunch parsley
- 1 carrot
- 1 cup Swiss chard
- 2 radishes
- 2 tomatoes
- Tabasco, to taste

Procedure:

1. Juice the ingredients, putting in water as required.

JACKFRUIT TREAT

Time to prepare: **Approximately ten minutes**

Yield: 2 Servings

What You'll Need:

- 1 cup jackfruit
- 1 grapefruit, peeled
- 1 handful sunflower sprouts
- 1 lemon, peeled
- 4 Brussels sprouts

Procedure:

1. Juice the ingredients and serve it instantly.

KALE AND PEAR JUICE WITH GRAPES

Time to prepare: **Approximately ten minutes**

Yield: 2 Servings

What You'll Need:

- 1 bunch green grapes
- 2 carrots, trimmed
- 2 pears
- 4 kale leaves

Procedure:

1. Juice the ingredients using a juice extractor.
2. Pour into tall chilled glasses.

KIWI AND GRAPEFRUIT JUICE

Time to prepare: **Approximately ten minutes**

Yield: 2 Servings

What You'll Need:

- 1 pear, cored
- 1/2 cup coconut water
- 2 pink grapefruits, peeled and seeded
- 3 kiwi fruits, peeled

Procedure:

1. Juice all of the above ingredients.
2. Pour the juice into glasses before you serve.

KIWI-APPLE DELIGHT

Time to prepare: Approximately ten minutes

Yield: 2 Servings

What You'll Need:

- 2 apples, cored and diced
- 2 big handfuls spinach
- 2 kiwis, peeled

Procedure:

1. Push all ingredients through a juicer in accordance with manufacturer's recommendations.
2. Best enjoyed chilled.

LEAN JUICE

Time to prepare: Approximately ten minutes

Yield: 2 Servings

What You'll Need:

- 1 small bitter melon
- 1 apple
- 2 carrots
- 1 lemon
- 1/2 small pineapple

Procedure:

1. Rinse all ingredients thoroughly.
2. Next, remove the skin from the melon and pineapple. Chop the melon in half and scoop out the seeds. Core the apple and scrub the carrots.
3. Push everything through juicer and serve!

LETTUCE AND BLACKBERRY DELIGHT

Time to prepare: Approximately ten minutes

Yield: 2 Servings

What You'll Need:

- 1 banana, peeled
- 1 cup blackberries
- 1/2 lime, juiced
- 2 cups lettuce greens

Procedure:

1. Blend lettuce and blackberries until the desired smoothness is achieved.
2. Put in water and the rest of the ingredients.

LOTUS ROOT AND TANGERINE JUICE

Time to prepare: Approximately ten minutes

Yield: 2 Servings

What You'll Need:

- 1 carrot
- 1 section of lotus root
- 1-inch ginger
- 4 tangerines

Procedure:

1. Peel lotus root, scrub the carrot, and take the rind off tangerine and ginger root.
2. Juice the ingredients and serve immediately!

MEDITERRANEAN JUICE

Time to prepare: Approximately ten minutes

Yield: 2 Servings

What You'll Need:

- 1 beet
- 1 big cucumber
- 1 lemon, peeled
- 1 teaspoon olive oil
- 1 tomato
- 2 celery ribs

Procedure:

1. Simply throw the ingredients into your juicer. Juice the ingredients and move them to serving glasses.
2. Shake before you serve.

MELON AND COCONUT JUICE

Time to prepare: Approximately ten minutes

Yield: 2 Servings

What You'll Need:

- 1 cup watermelon chunks
- 1 tangerine, peeled
- 1/2 cup coconut water
- 1/2 honeydew melon, peeled

Procedure:

1. Juice all the ingredients; move the juice to the glasses.

MINT PINEAPPLE JUICE

Time to prepare: **Approximately ten minutes**

Yield: 2 Servings

What You'll Need:

- 1 cup pineapple, peeled and slice into chunks
- 1 tablespoon mint leaves
- 2 celery stalks, with leaves

Procedure:

1. Process the pineapple and celery through a juicer.
2. Serve the juice decorated with mint leaves.

MINTY BEETS WITH FRUITS

Time to prepare: **Approximately ten minutes**

Yield: 2 Servings

What You'll Need:

- 1 big cucumber
- 1 handful parsley
- 1 orange, peeled and segmented
- 1 pear, cored
- 2 sugar beets including greens
- 2 tablespoons fresh mint leaves

Procedure:

1. Process the beets with greens through a juicer.
2. Put in the rest of the ingredients.
3. Blend your juice meticulously to blend; serve over ice and enjoy.

MINTY WATERMELON TREAT

Time to prepare: Approximately ten minutes

Yield: 2 Servings

What You'll Need:

- 1 handful mint
- 1 tomato
- 1/4 medium watermelon
- A pinch of kosher salt

Procedure:

1. Take the rind off watermelon.
2. Push all of the above ingredients through the juicer. Pour into two chilled glasses.

MOUTH-WATERING DRINK

Time to prepare: Approximately ten minutes

Yield: 2 Servings

What You'll Need:

- 1 celery rib
- 1 head lettuce
- 1/2 pineapple
- A thumb-sized piece of ginger

Procedure:

1. Juice all the above ingredients and serve in two thoroughly chilled glasses.

ORANGE BLUEBERRY BLAST

Time to prepare: Approximately ten minutes

Yield: 2 Servings

What You'll Need:

- 1 cup blueberries
- 1 large-sized banana, peeled
- 1 orange, peeled

Procedure:

1. Process the orange and blueberries through a juicer according to the manufacturer's instructions.

2. Put in the banana and move everything to a blender; blend until a smooth and consistent mixture is achieved. Serve as soon as you can.

ORANGE INVIGORATION

Time to prepare: **Approximately ten minutes**

Yield: 2 Servings

What You'll Need:

- 1 orange
- 1 sweet potato
- 2 apples
- 2 carrots
- A dash pumpkin pie spice

Procedure:

1. Simply put in the ingredients to your juicer. Push the ingredients and pour the juice into glasses.
2. Drizzle some extra pumpkin pie spice on the top.

ORANGE-CARROT CRUSH

Time to prepare: **Approximately ten minutes**

Yield: 2 Servings

What You'll Need:

- 1 orange, peeled
- 4 big carrots, trimmed

Procedure:

1. Process all ingredients through a juicer.

PAPAYA AND STRAWBERRY JUICE

Time to prepare: Approximately ten minutes

Yield: 2 Servings

What You'll Need:

- 1 cup strawberries, hulled
- 1 tablespoon fresh mint
- 1/2 cup raspberries
- 2 papayas

Procedure:

1. Process the ingredients through your electronic juicer in accordance with the manufacturer's instructions.
2. Stir or shake juice before you serve.

PARTY GINGER DRINK

Time to prepare: Approximately ten minutes

Yield: 2 Servings

What You'll Need:

- 1 ½ cups water, or as required to cover
- 1/2 cup honey
- 1/3 pound fresh ginger root, unpeeled
- 4 big lemons, juiced
- 6 cups water
- Fresh mint, to taste

Procedure:

1. Put ginger and water into a blender; blend until the mixture is pasty.
2. Strain the juice from ginger mixture into a pitcher. Put in the remaining ingredients and stir until blended.

PEACH AND RASPBERRY JUICE

Time to prepare: Approximately ten minutes

Yield: 4 Servings

What You'll Need:

- 1 ½" ginger
- 10 raspberries
- 2 apricots, pitted
- 3 peaches, pitted

- A dash of Chinese 5-spice

Procedure:

1. Put in all ingredients through your juice extractor. Serve over crushed ice.

PEAR AND LETTUCE JUICE

Time to prepare: Approximately ten minutes

Yield: 2 Servings

What You'll Need:

- 1 cucumber
- 1 pear
- 1" ginger
- 1/2 teaspoon allspice
- 3 leaves Iceberg lettuce
- 4 carrots

Procedure:

1. Trim the carrot, torn the lettuce leaves, core the pear, and peel ginger root.
2. Process all ingredients through your juicer and serve thoroughly chilled!

PEAR AND YAM DELIGHT

Time to prepare: **Approximately ten minutes**

Yield: **2 Servings**

What You'll Need:

- 1 moderate-sized yam, peeled
- 1/2 teaspoon vanilla extract
- 2 carrots, trimmed
- 3 pears, cored

Procedure:

1. To start, process the pears through a juicer in accordance with the manufacturer's instructions.
2. Put in the carrots, followed by the yam and vanilla extract. Shake before you serve.

PEAR-CABBAGE JUICE

Time to prepare: **Approximately ten minutes**

Yield: **2 Servings**

What You'll Need:

- 1 large-sized green apple, cored
- 1 pear, cored
- 1 small-sized lime

- 1/2 teaspoon allspice
- 1/4 cup cabbage

Procedure:

1. Rinse all ingredients meticulously.
2. Now process all ingredients through a juicer in accordance with manufacturer's recommendations. Pour into two glasses and serve with straws.

PEAR-TANGERINE BLAST

Time to prepare: Approximately ten minutes

Yield: 2 Servings

What You'll Need:

- 1 apple, cored
- 1 big carrot, trimmed
- 1 ripe pear, cored
- 1 sweet potato, peeled and diced
- 2 medium tangerines, peeled

Procedure:

1. Rinse the ingredients meticulously.
2. Push the carrot and sweet potato through your juicer according to the manufacturer's instructions.

3. Put in the apple, pear, and tangerine segments; process again and serve immediately.

PINEAPPLE BLUEBERRY JUICE

Time to prepare: Approximately ten minutes

Yield: 2 Servings

What You'll Need:

- 1 cup blueberries
- 1 tablespoon fresh mint leaves
- 1/2 medium pineapple
- 2 oranges

Procedure:

1. To start, take the rind off pineapple and oranges. Next, move them to a juice extractor. Put in the rest of the above ingredients.
2. Process the ingredients until they are meticulously mixed. Pour the juice into glasses.

PINEAPPLE MELON JUICE

Time to prepare: Approximately ten minutes

Yield: 3 Servings

What You'll Need:

- 1 beetroot
- 2 carrots
- 2 celery ribs
- 1/2 moderate-sized pineapple
- 1/2-inch ginger root
- 1/4 moderate-sized melon

Procedure:

1. Take the rind off pineapple and melon. Peel the beetroot and ginger root, and scrub the carrots.
2. Next, clean all ingredients.
3. Put in everything through a juicer and serve immediately!

PINEAPPLE-GINGER CLEANSER

Time to prepare: **Approximately ten minutes**

Yield: 2 Servings

What You'll Need:

- 1 lemon
- 1 orange, peeled
- 1" ginger, peeled and grated
- 1/2 medium pineapple, rind removed

Procedure:

1. Push all of the above ingredients through the juicer.
2. Pour into a couple of glasses.

PLUM AND PEAR JUICE

Time to prepare: Approximately ten minutes

Yield: 1 Serving

What You'll Need:

- 1 pear
- 1" ginger
- 1/2 beet
- 2 carrots
- 4 leaves spinach
- 4 plums, pitted

Procedure:

1. Juice the ingredients and serve immediately!

PLUM TOMATO JUICE

Time to prepare: Approximately ten minutes

Yield: 2 Servings

What You'll Need:

- 1 bell pepper, seeded
- 1 fennel
- 1 small handful parsley
- 1 teaspoon coconut oil
- 1/2 lemon, peeled
- 3 plum tomatoes
- A pinch of dried oregano
- A pinch sea salt

Procedure:

1. Rinse all ingredients meticulously.
2. Push all of the above ingredients through the juicer. Adjust the seasonings to taste.

POMEGRANATE WATERMELON JUICE

Time to prepare: Approximately ten minutes

Yield: 2 Servings

What You'll Need:

- 1 cup pomegranate seeds
- 1/3 medium watermelon
- 12 strawberries
- 4 sprigs mint

Procedure:

1. Take the rind off watermelon.
2. Put in all ingredients through your juice machine.

POST-WORKOUT REVITALIZER

Time to prepare: Approximately ten minutes

Yield: 1 Serving

What You'll Need:

- 1 apple, cored and cubed
- 1 carrot, scrubbed and crudely chopped
- 1 small sweet potato, scrubbed and crudely chopped
- 1/2 cup water
- 1/4 cup raw almonds
- 2 oranges, peeled and slice into chunks

Procedure:

1. In a blender, mix all the above ingredients: then; blend, scraping down sides, until uniform and smooth.
2. Strain juice and put in some extra water if required. The ingredients help you build and repair your muscles. Enjoy!

PROTEIN SPIRULINA LIMEADE

Time to prepare: Approximately ten minutes

Yield: 2 Servings

What You'll Need:

- 1 apple
- 1 bunch watercress
- 1 lime, peeled
- 1 nectarine
- 1 pear
- 1 tablespoon spirulina powder

Procedure:

1. Simply put in all the ingredients to your juicer.
2. Juice and serve in thoroughly chilled glasses.

PURPLE KALE AND CARROT JUICE

Time to prepare: Approximately ten minutes

Yield: 2 Servings

What You'll Need:

- 1 green garlic
- 1 lemon, peeled
- 1 red bell pepper
- 3 carrots
- 4 leaves purple kale
- 45–50 drops Echinacea

Procedure:

1. Juice all the ingredients, apart from for Echinacea.
2. Put in Echinacea and mix to blend. Pour into glasses.

RADICCHIO AND LEMON DELIGHT

Time to prepare: Approximately ten minutes

Yield: 2 Servings

What You'll Need:

- 1 cup spinach, torn into pieces
- 1 green apple, cored
- 1 handful radicchio
- 1 lime, peeled
- 1 teaspoon lemon zest
- 2 carrots, trimmed
- 3 radishes

Procedure:

1. Rinse the ingredients and then, cut them to sizes that fit your juice extractor.
2. Finally, juice them and serve it in a couple of glasses.

RADISH AND PEPPER JUICE

Time to prepare: Approximately ten minutes

Yield: 2 Servings

What You'll Need:

- 1 bell pepper
- 1 lime
- 1 tomato
- 1-inch ginger root
- 3 carrots
- 4 red radishes

Procedure:

1. Juice the ingredients and serve immediately.

RAINBOW JUICE

Time to prepare: Approximately ten minutes

Yield: 2 Servings

What You'll Need:

- 1 handful mint
- 1 kiwi, peeled
- 1 lemon, peeled
- 1/2 rock melon
- 12 strawberries
- 2 plums

Procedure:

1. Juice the ingredients and serve over crushed ice.

RED CABBAGE JUICE

Time to prepare: **Approximately ten minutes**

Yield: **2 Servings**

What You'll Need:

- 1 apple, cored
- 1 lemon, peeled
- 1 pear, cored
- 1 small-sized head red cabbage
- 4 carrots

Procedure:

1. Juice all the ingredients. Serve over ice cubes if you wish.

ROOT VEGETABLE DETOX

Time to prepare: **Approximately ten minutes**

Yield: **2 Servings**

What You'll Need:

- 1-inch fresh ginger root
- 3 beets

- 3 carrots
- 3 stalks celery

Procedure:

1. Process all ingredients using a juice extractor.
2. Pour into two thoroughly chilled tall glasses.

SIMPLE DETOXING BLEND

Time to prepare: **Approximately ten minutes**

Yield: 2 Servings

What You'll Need:

- 1 bunch parsley
- 1 medium apple, cored
- 1 medium cucumber
- Water to make 1 cup juice

Procedure:

1. Juice all the above ingredients. Enjoy!!

SIMPLE FRUIT AND VEGGIE JUICE

Time to prepare: **Approximately ten minutes**

Yield: 1 Serving

What You'll Need:

- 1 apple, cored and quartered
- 1 carrot, trimmed
- 1 handful parsley
- 1 orange, peeled
- 1/2 head red cabbage, wrapped into balls

Procedure:

1. To start, wash your ingredients meticulously. Push all the ingredients through your juicer.
2. Serve in your punch container if you wish.

SIMPLE REJUVINATOR

Time to prepare: **Approximately ten minutes**

Yield: **1 Serving**

What You'll Need:

- 1 cucumber
- 2 Roma tomatoes
- A pinch of Himalayan salt

Procedure:

1. Juice all the ingredients. Salt isn't necessary.

SIP OF INDIA

Time to prepare: Approximately ten minutes

Yield: 2 Servings

What You'll Need:

- 1/2 lemon
- 2 apples
- 2 pears
- 2" ginger
- A dash of Garam masala

Procedure:

1. Core the apples and pears. Take the rind off lemon and ginger. Move the ingredients to your juicer. Put in Garam masala.
2. Pour into two glasses and serve immediately!

SOFT SUMMER JUICE

Time to prepare: Approximately ten minutes

Yield: 2 Servings

What You'll Need:

- 1 cup blueberries
- 1 tablespoon fresh mint leaves

- 1/2 cup pomegranate seeds
- 1/4 medium watermelon

Procedure:

1. To start, take the rind off watermelon.
2. Rinse the ingredients and put in them through a juicer. Serve thoroughly chilled.

SPICE BLAST

Time to prepare: Approximately ten minutes

Yield: 2 Servings

What You'll Need:

- 1 cucumber
- 1 small-sized red onion, peeled
- 1 orange, peeled
- A dash cayenne pepper
- 1/2 jicama, peeled
- 1/2 bell pepper

Procedure:

1. Rinse all your ingredients and move them to a juice extractor.
2. Pour the juice into glasses. Sprinkle with some extra cayenne pepper.

SPICY DANDELION GREENS JUICE

Time to prepare: Approximately ten minutes

Yield: 2 Servings

What You'll Need:

- 1 bulb radicchio
- 1 bunch dandelion greens
- 1 bunch fresh cilantro
- 1 lime
- A dash of cayenne pepper

Procedure:

1. Process the ingredients in your juicer in accordance with manufacturer's directions.

SPICY ROOT VEGETABLE JUICE

Time to prepare: Approximately ten minutes

Yield: 2 Servings

What You'll Need:

- 1 beet, scrubbed and chopped
- 1/2 cup water
- 1/4 teaspoon cloves
- 2 moderate-sized apples, cored and diced

- 2 tablespoons fresh ginger, peeled and chopped
- 3 large-sized carrots, scrubbed and cut

Procedure:

1. In a blender, mix all the above ingredients and blend until the desired smoothness is achieved.
2. Strain juice; you can put in an additional 1/2 cup of water if you wish. Shake before you serve and serve with drinking straws.

SPICY TANGY CUCUMBER JUICE

Time to prepare: Approximately ten minutes

Yield: 1 Serving

What You'll Need:

- 1 clove garlic, peeled
- 1 cucumber
- 1 teaspoon dried dill weed
- 2 key limes
- 2 scallions, trimmed

Procedure:

1. Process your ingredients through a juicer in accordance with the manufacturer's directions.

2. Stir before you serve and serve over ice cubes if you wish.

SPINACH POWER

Time to prepare: Approximately ten minutes

Yield: 2 Servings

What You'll Need:

- 1 cup raspberries
- 1 orange
- 2 bunches spinach
- 2 cups pineapple

Procedure:

1. Put the ingredients into your juice extractor.
2. Juice the ingredients and serve in glasses.

SPINACH-CARROT JUICE

Time to prepare: Approximately ten minutes

Yield: 2 Servings

What You'll Need:

- 1 bunch parsley
- 2 apples

- 2 carrots
- 2 handfuls spinach

Procedure:

1. To start, rinse all the ingredients meticulously.
2. Push all of the above ingredients through the juicer before you serve.

SUMMER FROSTBITE

Time to prepare: Approximately fifteen minutes

Yield: 2 Servings

What You'll Need:

- 1-inch ginger
- 1/2 medium watermelon
- 1/2 medium pineapple
- 1/4 teaspoon Maca powder

Procedure:

1. Take the rind off watermelon and pineapple. Put in them to the juicer.
2. Mix in Maca powder and ginger; process the ingredients in the juicer.

SUMMERTIME MINT JUICE

Time to prepare: Approximately fifteen minutes

Yield: 2 Servings

What You'll Need:

- 1 apple
- 1 celery rib
- 1 handful mint leaves
- 1/2 cup strawberries
- 2 handfuls spinach

Procedure:

1. Put the ingredients into a juicer.
2. Pour the juice into the glasses.

SWEET CAULIFLOWER DELIGHT

Time to prepare: Approximately ten minutes

Yield: 2 Servings

What You'll Need:

- 1 apple
- 1 carrot
- 1 celery rib
- 1 moderate-sized head cauliflower

- 2 oranges, peeled

Procedure:

1. Push all of the above ingredients through the juicer.
2. Pour into two chilled glasses.

SWEET POTATO TREAT

Time to prepare: **Approximately ten minutes**

Yield: **2 Servings**

What You'll Need:

- 1 celery rib
- 1 lemon, peeled
- 1 medium sweet potato, peeled
- 1-inch piece ginger
- 2 kiwis
- 4 medium carrots, trimmed

Procedure:

1. Push the sweet potatoes and carrots through a juicer according to the manufacturer's instructions.
2. Put in the kiwis, followed by the ginger, lemon, and celery rib.

TAKE-OFF

Time to prepare: Approximately ten minutes

Yield: 2 Servings

What You'll Need:

- 1 apple
- 1 cucumber
- 1 kiwi fruit
- 1 lemon
- 1/2 cup sprouts
- 4 carrots

Procedure:

1. Process all ingredients using a juice extractor.
2. Pour the juice into a couple of glasses.

TANGERINE AND GINGER JUICE

Time to prepare: Approximately ten minutes

Yield: 2 Servings

What You'll Need:

- 1 small-sized lime
- 1-inch ginger root
- 4 tangerines

Procedure:

1. Juice all the ingredients and serve it instantly.

TANGERINE AND ROOT VEGETABLES WITH GREENS

Time to prepare: Approximately ten minutes

Yield: 2 Servings

What You'll Need:

- 1 bunch watercress
- 1 cup spinach leaves
- 1 green apple
- 1 small beet
- 1/4 teaspoon cumin seeds
- 2 carrots
- 2 tangerines
- Fresh ginger to taste

Procedure:

1. Peel your tangerines and core the apples. Torn greens, scrub the carrot, and peel the beetroot.
2. Put in the ingredients to your juice maker.
3. Serve thoroughly chilled and enjoy!

TANGERINE DELIGHT

Time to prepare: **Approximately fifteen minutes**

Yield: **4 Servings**

What You'll Need:

- 1 small beetroot
- 1/2 teaspoon Maca powder
- 1/2" ginger
- 4 carrots
- 4 tangerines

Procedure:

1. Peel the tangerines but leave the white pith. Juice the tangerines and move the juice to the blender.
2. Put in the carrots, beetroot, ginger, and Maca powder. Blend until the desired smoothness is achieved.
3. Serve immediately and enjoy!

TANGERINE TURMERIC JUICE

Time to prepare: **Approximately ten minutes**

Yield: **2 Servings**

What You'll Need:

- 1-inch fresh turmeric

- 2 tangerines
- 3 carrots
- 3 stalks celery

Procedure:

1. Rinse all ingredients; then, process them using a juice extractor.

TANGERINE-CARROT CRUSH

Time to prepare: Approximately ten minutes

Yield: 2 Servings

What You'll Need:

- 1/2" ginger root
- 1/4 teaspoon cloves
- 4 carrots
- 4 tangerines

Procedure:

1. Trim the carrots, and peel tangerines and ginger root. Next, wash the ingredients and move them to your juicer.
2. Next, put in cloves and juice all the ingredients. Enjoy!

TROPICAL GREEN DELIGHT

Time to prepare: **Approximately ten minutes**

Yield: **2 Servings**

What You'll Need:

- 1 cup coconut water
- 1 cup pineapple
- 1 medium Granny Smith apple
- 1 pear
- 1/2 pink grapefruit, peeled and seeded
- 1/4 cup parsley
- 2 handfuls spinach leaves

Procedure:

1. Take the rind off pineapple and chop the fruit into chunks. Core the apple and the pear. Tear spinach leaves and parsley.
2. Finally, peel red grapefruit. Put in all the ingredients to your juice extractor together with coconut water.
3. Process them until you get the juice. Pour into glasses and drizzle with some extra coconut flakes if you wish. Enjoy!

TROPICAL MINT BLAST

Time to prepare: **Approximately ten minutes**

Yield: 3 Servings

What You'll Need:

- 1 cup strawberries
- 1 mango, peeled and cored
- 1 tablespoon mint leaves
- 1 teaspoon fresh grated ginger
- 1/4 cup pineapple, peeled and slice into chunks
- 2 apricots, pitted

Procedure:

1. Process the ingredients through your electronic juicer according to the manufacturer's instructions.
2. You can make the juice sweeter with the raw honey.

ULTIMATE TOMATO JUICE

Time to prepare: Approximately ten minutes

Yield: 2 Servings

What You'll Need:

- 1 bell pepper, seeded
- 1 cucumber
- 1 lime
- 1 tomato
- 3 carrots

Procedure:

1. Rinse all ingredients meticulously.
2. Next, put in all ingredients through a juicer. Serve in individual glasses and enjoy!

ULTRA GREEN DELIGHT

Time to prepare: Approximately ten minutes

Yield: 2 Servings

What You'll Need:

- 1 cucumber
- 1 lemon cut into four equivalent portions, peeled
- 1 tomato
- 2 cups fresh green beans
- 5 big leaves lettuce

Procedure:

1. To start, press the beans through your electronic juicer.
2. Mix in the lettuce, followed by the cucumber, tomato, and the lemon.
3. Combine the juice meticulously and serve instantly.

ULTRA WINTER MIX

Time to prepare: Approximately ten minutes

Yield: 2 Servings

What You'll Need:

- 1 handful alfalfa sprouts
- 1 handful watercress
- 1/2 lime
- 1/2-inch chunk of broccoli stem
- 2 carrots
- 2 Royal Gala apples

Procedure:

1. Juice all the above ingredients.
2. Next, pour the juice over ice and drink immediately!

UPLIFTING SPICY JUICE

Time to prepare: Approximately fifteen minutes

Yield: 4 Servings

What You'll Need:

- 1 cucumber
- 1 jalapeño pepper, seeded
- 1 whole lime
- 1/2 teaspoon allspice
- 1/4 cup kale leaves
- 3 celery ribs

Procedure:

1. Peel cucumber and lime. Move them to your juicer together with the rest of the ingredients.
2. Push all ingredients through your juicer. Serve immediately with bendy straws and enjoy!

VEGGIE STIMULATOR

Time to prepare: Approximately ten minutes

Yield: 2 Servings

What You'll Need:

- 1 cup spinach
- 1 small cucumber
- 1 small tangerine
- 1/2 lemon, peeled
- 1/4 bulb fennel
- 1/4 inch ginger,
- 2 pears, cored

Procedure:

1. Core the pears and process them through the feed tube of your electronic juicer.
2. Put the rest of the ingredients and mix your juice meticulously.
3. Finally, serve over crushed ice if you wish.

VEGGIE-LIME DELIGHT

Time to prepare: Approximately ten minutes

Yield: 1 Serving

What You'll Need:

- 1 big cucumber
- 1/2 lime, peeled
- 1/2 cup parsley
- 2 cloves garlic, peeled

Procedure:

1. Process the cucumber, garlic, and parsley through a juicer.
2. Serve over ice cubes if you wish.

VEGGIE-SPROUT BLAST

Time to prepare: Approximately ten minutes

Yield: 2 Servings

What You'll Need:

- 1 cucumber
- 1/2 cup alfalfa sprouts
- 2 carrots
- 2 handfuls fresh spinach

- 6 leaves Iceberg lettuce

Procedure:

1. To start, process carrots and cucumber through a juicer. Next, put in the lettuce leaves to the feeding tube.
2. Put in the spinach and sprouts. Mix your juice meticulously and serve with drinking straws. Enjoy!

WATERMELON AND GINGER JUICE

Time to prepare: Approximately ten minutes

Yield: 4 Servings

What You'll Need:

- 1" ginger
- 1/2 medium watermelon
- 1/2 medium pineapple

Procedure:

1. Put in all ingredients through your juicer.
2. Pour thoroughly chilled juice into a couple of glasses and enjoy!

WHEATGRASS AND ARUGULA JUICE

Time to prepare: Approximately ten minutes

Yield: 2 Servings

What You'll Need:

- 2 handfuls arugula
- 2 oranges, peeled
- 2 ounces wheatgrass

Procedure:

1. Push the ingredients using a juice extractor.
2. Serve over crushed ice if you wish.

WHEATGRASS TANGY DELIGHT

Time to prepare: Approximately ten minutes

Yield: 2 Servings

What You'll Need:

- 1 lime
- 2 grapefruits
- 2 sprigs rosemary
- 3 oranges
- 30 tablespoons wheatgrass juice

Procedure:

1. Put all the ingredients into your blender; mix thoroughly and pour into the glasses.

WINTER BLAST

Time to prepare: Approximately ten minutes

Yield: 2 Servings

What You'll Need:

- 1/2 teaspoon cinnamon powder
- 1/4 teaspoon grated nutmeg
- 1-inch ginger
- 2 apples
- 3 carrots

Procedure:

1. Trim the carrots, core the apples and peel ginger root. Now rinse all the ingredients.
2. Put in the ingredients through a juicer.
3. Pour prepared juice into 2 thoroughly chilled glasses. Shake before you serve and try to drink instantly.

WINTER TREASURE

Time to prepare: Approximately ten minutes

Yield: 1 Serving

What You'll Need:

- 1 jicama, peeled

- 1 orange, peeled
- 1 tablespoon mint
- 1/4 teaspoon ground cloves
- 1/4 teaspoon turmeric
- 2 sprigs coriander

Procedure:

1. Rinse all your ingredients meticulously.
2. Push the ingredients through a juicer and enjoy! Can be enjoyed hot or cold.

YAM-PINEAPPLE DELIGHT

Time to prepare: Approximately ten minutes

Yield: 2 Servings

What You'll Need:

- 1 small-sized pineapple
- 1 yam, peeled
- 1/2 teaspoon Maca powder
- 2 carrots, trimmed
- 4 tangerines, peeled

Procedure:

1. Process yam through your electronic juicer according to the manufacturer's instructions.

2. Put in tangerine and carrots.
3. Take the rind off pineapple. Chop it into slices and move to the juicer. Next, put in Maca powder. Juice all the ingredients and pour prepared juice into a couple of glasses. Enjoy!

YAM-TANGERINE REFRESH

Time to prepare: Approximately ten minutes

Yield: 2 Servings

What You'll Need:

- 1 yam, peeled
- 2 pears, cored
- 4 tangerines, peeled

Procedure:

1. Simply put all ingredients into your juicer.
2. Serve thoroughly chilled and enjoy.
3. This is a carbohydrate-rich juice so it boosts your energy instantly.

YUMMY PURPLE JUICE

Time to prepare: Approximately fifteen minutes

Yield: 2 Servings

What You'll Need:

- 1 beetroot
- 1 large-sized jicama
- 1/2 bunch parsley
- 1/2-inch ginger root
- 1/4 lemon, with peel

Procedure:

1. Process all ingredients using a juice extractor.
2. Pour into two tall glasses and serve immediately.

ENDNOTE

Thank you for your time. I hope you found a few recipes in this book that you absolutely loved, and will enjoy for the rest of your life!

Good Luck, stay safe, stay healthy, and have fun!

Printed in Great Britain
by Amazon